Prehistoric Britain

I.H. LONGWORTH

Published for
The Trustees of the British Museum by
BRITISH MUSEUM PRESS

© 1985 The Trustees of the British Museum
Second impression, 1991

ISBN 0 7141 2037 5

Published by British Museum Press
a division of British Museum Publications Limited
46 Bloomsbury Street, London WC1B 3QQ

Designed and produced by Roger Davies

Printed in Italy by New Interlitho

THE TRUSTEES OF THE BRITISH MUSEUM acknowledge with gratitude the generosity of THE HENRY MOORE FOUNDATION for the grant which made possible the publication of this book.

Front cover. Standing stones at Avebury, Wiltshire.

Inside front cover. Aerial photograph of the hillfort of Maiden Castle, Dorset showing multiple ramparts and complex entrances.

Title page. Detail of a bronze flesh hook from Dunaverney, Co. Antrim (see fig. 73).

This page. A range of Beaker pottery (from the left) from Hemp Knoll, Bishops Cannings, Wiltshire; Rudstone, Humberside; Goodmanham, Humberside; Lambourn, Berkshire and Hitchin, Hertfordshire.

Back cover. One of the three Folkton Drums (see fig. 35).

Contents

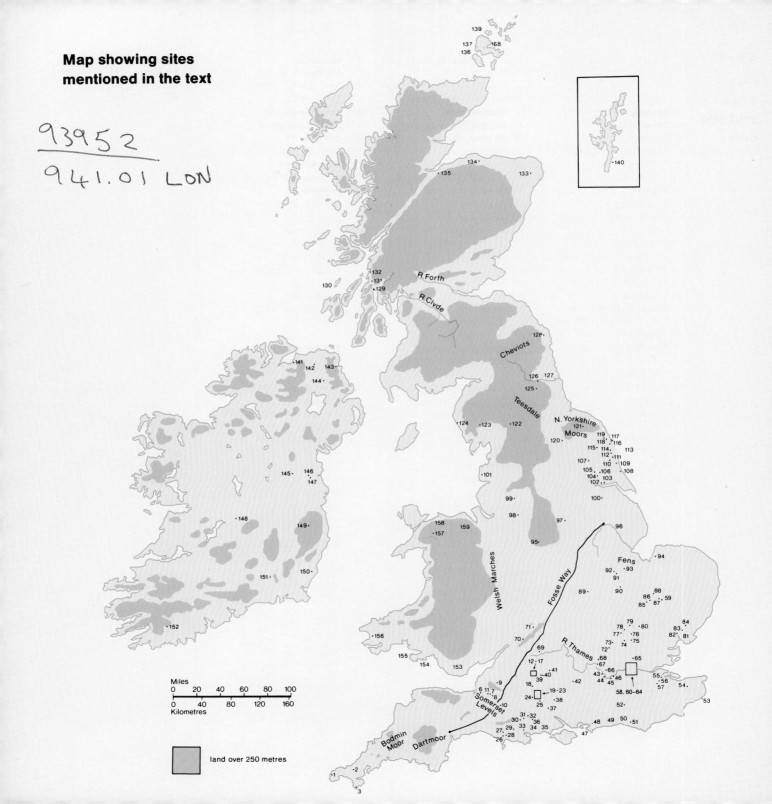

**Map showing sites
mentioned in the text**

93952
941.01 LON

R. Forth

R. Clyde

Cheviots

Teesdale

N. Yorkshire
Moors

Welsh Marches

Fosse Way

Fens

R. Thames

Somerset
Levels

Bodmin
Moor

Dartmoor

Miles
0   20   40   60   80   100
0   40   80   120 160
Kilometres

land over 250 metres

Key to Map of sites and site index

Illustration numbers appear in bold type

Introduction: a question of time and other problems

To understand the remote past is not an easy task, for to do so we must also understand time. Living in an age when in each year major advances in technology occur with amazing regularity, it is difficult to appreciate a more distant age when technological change can barely be detected over tens of thousands of years. As we approach the present day the speed of change quickens, but in Britain it is not until the Roman era that individual years take on real significance. For much of the prehistoric period, when no form of written record survives, we must rely on a different form of chronometer – radioactive decay – and talk not in calendar but in radiocarbon years. Fortunately all living things contain carbon and in particular a radioactive isotope carbon 14. When the organism dies no new carbon is absorbed and the radioactive isotope begins to decay at a known rate. By comparing the amount of radiocarbon remaining with the known constant percentage present in all living matter, the age of the substance to be dated can be determined. Save for the most remote periods carbon 14 provides our time-scale, a small bc being used to set these years apart from calendar dates. Without such guidance, time for the prehistorian would be like the proverbial piece of string.

A sense of time gives a sense of order but we face other problems. To describe the remains of the past is fairly simple but to appreciate their purpose or to gauge the value originally placed upon them can tax the imagination and often must lie beyond our grasp. What we observe now is through the eyes of the twentieth century and the way in which we interpret objects and situations may be remote from the perceptions of the age in which they were created. The further back in time we go, the less familiar things become and the more hazardous the use of rational explanation. Above all we must be aware of the unevenness of the evidence that survives. Only rarely will the right combination of factors be present to allow us to glimpse more than a partial picture of the past. The natural decay of wood and skin, of leather, cloth, rope and string gives a strangely lopsided look to the surviving evidence. Much of this we must consciously put back with our mind's eye so that the axe-head can fit firmly within its haft and the timber house rise from the post-holes and stains that alone survive in the ground.

We must remember also that, area for area, Britain possesses one of the most varied landscapes in the northern hemisphere. Few statements can be made with regard to modern life that are true of all places and every situation, and the same is yet more true of our prehistoric past. All that we can hope to offer in this book is a broad view of Britain's past, illustrated here and there by discoveries and objects drawn mainly from the British Museum's unrivalled collections illustrating some of the many aspects of achievement and variation which make our unwritten past a subject of constant fascination.

1 *far right*. Two flint handaxes from Swanscombe, Kent and Elveden, Suffolk. Larger handaxe 6.2 ins (15.7 cms)

2 A flint point and two scrapers from High Lodge, Suffolk. Length of largest scraper 4.7 in (11.9 cm)

Human predators

Man had already reached Britain up to half a million years ago. This was not modern man but a precursor and the appearance of the land was to change many times before it became the British Isles as we know them today, but the social history of Britain began when the first parties of human predators reached what was then the furthest extent of their European hunting territories. The massive climatic fluctuations which had brought successive periods of intensely cold weather interspersed with warmer phases to Europe over $c.800,000$ years dominated life. Man could only live in Britain during spells when the natural fauna and flora on which he depended could re-colonise and re-establish themselves. During the glacial periods, as massive quantities of water became locked away in ice, the sea level fell making large areas of the present North Sea dry land. In these phases Britain formed part of the European land mass. As warmer weather set in the ice began to recede and the rising sea level would have left the British Isles a group of islands as they are today. The process was repeated more than once. It was only between the extremes when the climate was tolerably warm but access not yet impossible that man reached Britain only to retreat before the onset of the next glacial maximum.

Our knowledge of these earliest episodes in our history remains rather sketchy. Much of the evidence has been destroyed or modified by later ice action and little survives beyond the stone tools and remains of the animals on which man fed. The seasonal cycle of animal, fish and bird migration on the one hand and the growth and ripening of plant and seed must have dominated existence, but in the absence of surviving traces it is difficult to assess just how dependent man was upon the floral element in his diet. Chances are however that for some parts of the year that dependence could have been near total.

The types of tool which man was making at this remote period to help in the food quest are fairly restricted. The handaxe was a multi-purpose tool, known to have been made and used for example at Boxgrove in West Sussex for horse-butchery – a tool to be kept for on-going use. Elsewhere at Clacton on the Essex coast and in Suffolk at Barnham and High Lodge flakes were used to meet specific short-term needs, some for cutting, others no doubt for whittling wood, and then discarded. In wood itself, little survives save a spear from Clacton. Yet the ability to shape natural materials into objects to assist in the basic needs of life was a crucial factor in man's success in adapting to the varied and often harsh conditions in which he was forced to live.

It is only towards the close of the glacial period that we can begin to flesh out the picture a little more clearly. During the last major period of glaciation between 120,000 and 8000 bc temperatures continued to fluctuate. During the milder spells rich grasslands gave grazing to wild horse, mammoth, bison and reindeer and in their wake came modern man *Homo sapiens sapiens*. It is to this period that our first deliberate human burial can be dated. The young man buried in the South Welsh cave of Paviland on the Gower Peninsula had been sprinkled with red ochre and with him had been placed ornaments made of shell and ivory. Most of the surviving evidence of the period also comes from caves but a few open air camping sites are known and we must assume that these, though more difficult to locate, would have been far more numerous.

The principal weapon used against the swift-footed game of the grasslands was the hunting spear tipped with a leaf-shaped point, the carcass being worked with flake and scraper. Later a more extensive tool kit was developed made on carefully struck blades to include single-edged knives, boring and engraving tools and light blade-end scrapers. Worked bone also survives and from sites like Aveline's Hole in Somerset and Kent's Cavern in Devon come bone harpoon heads, spatulae, bone points and even needles. Besides the heavier game of the plains, fish and water birds like the goose and swan were sought as

3 *below left*. Tool kit comprising (from left to right) burin, modified blade, awl, side and end scrapers all made on flint blades and bone needle from the Church Hole Cave, Cresswell Crags, Derbyshire. Length of longest blade 3.7 in (9.3 cm)

4 *below*. Two flint axes of the type known as 'Thames Picks'. Both from the River Thames. Length of lower axe 5.5 in (14.1 cm)

5 *right*. Reconstructed arrow-shaft with inset flint microliths – small segments of flint flakes or blades trimmed to form a range of points and barbs. Other forms are shown to the right. All from Star Carr, Yorkshire. Lengh of arrowtip 1.05 in (2.7 cm)

well as ptarmigan and grouse.

By 8000 bc temperatures were reaching levels close to those of today and the open tundra of the last cold snap was giving way finally to a more forested landscape. The birch was the first tree to gain a footing followed by pine and hazel before the full mixed oak forest, dominated by elm, oak and lime, became established. With the return of the forest the animal population changed too in favour of woodland species like red and roe deer, elk, wild ox and wild boar. The warmer conditions which had caused progressive shrinkage of the ice mantle lead in turn both to a rise in sea level and, in the north, to a rise in the land which had become compressed beneath the weight of the accumulated ice above. These factors had three important results. In the south and east early coastal settlements would have become submerged beneath the rising water level while in the north comparable shoreline settlements have been lifted and now stand on former beachlines twelve metres above *OD*. The third, and for Britain most dramatic result, was that by 6,500 bc the sea had severed once and for all the last land-link with the Continent and from this time on Britain was to remain an island, often in contact with but never again forming part of the European land mass.

Before this final severance, contacts between Britain and Northern Europe had remained close. Over most of this area change to warm forested conditions with increased coverage of river, lake and bog had been met by a new range of hunting weaponry better suited to these conditions. Wood now becomes a major material, though one often to be inferred from other surviving evidence. This takes the form of the first hafted axes and 4 small, finely worked, pieces of flint – microliths 5 – which formed the point and barbs of wooden arrows, spears and harpoons. Bone and red deer antler was also increasingly worked and where waterlogged conditions have favoured preservation an impressive range of tools and implements survive. The most elegant of these weapons are the bone and antler points with barbs notched into one side. Many of these are 6 likely to have served as the points for fish spears but others were certainly used to point arrows as a chance discovery from Lancashire graphically reveals.

At Little Carlton near Poulton le Fylde the body of an elk was discovered preserved in a waterlogged deposit. Its lower body and limbs carried no fewer than seventeen wounds. Many of these had been made with flint tipped arrows but others were the result of axe-blows. In addition, part of a barbed bone point still lay lodged in the left hind foot. The elk had clearly been hunted and attacked at close quarters but had escaped only to die in a pool perhaps falling through the ice and becoming trapped beneath it.

Two of the most revealing sites from this period are also in northern Britain: Star Carr in North Yorkshire and Oronsay off the west coast of Scotland. The site at Star Carr lay on what was then the edge of a reed swamp fringing a lake. A rough but substantial floor of untrimmed birchwood had been laid down on the surface of the swamp to form a platform. Here we can trace a number of different activities, many connected with the dismemberment and later working of red deer carcasses. Much effort had gone into the making of barbed points from the antler, and skin-working tools show that hides were also being prepared on site. A series of stag frontlets 7 with portions of antler still attached had been worked into masks to help in stalking the deer. Other forest animals were also hunted from roe deer, elk, ox and wild pig down to hedgehog, fox and badger. The site was of course well placed for the hunting and snaring of water fowl and fishing but it is clear from the surviving remains that a wide range of plant

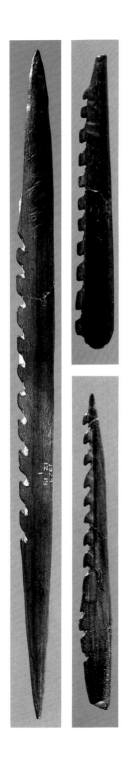

6 Points made from antler with barbs cut into one side from Royston, Hertfordshire, Hornsea and Skipsea, Humberside. Longest 10 ins (25.3 cm)

7 Stag frontlet and mattock head made of elk antler from Star Carr, Yorkshire. The frontlet is shown from the top to reveal the four holes made for its attachment probably to a hood of leather or skin. Length of mattock 7.9 in (20 cm)

food also made a substantial contribution to the diet. It was no doubt in this connection that a series of mattock heads made from elk antler was used.

The Star Carr site was probably but one of a number of places visited during the course of the year by a group of hunter-gatherers to exploit the seasonal sources of food within the area and to carry out specific manufacturing tasks. In all but the most favoured areas the need to move to survive must have been pressing. Recent work on Oronsay has given a particularly clear picture of this way of life. Here on a small Scottish island less than six square kilometres in extent it has been possible to trace how a small group of coastal hunter-gatherers living around 3500 bc moved from one to another of four or five separate sites to exploit the resources of the island and its coastal seas at different seasons of the year.

The land offered red deer, otter, plants and nuts; the sea, a variety of fish, especially the coalfish, seal and crab, while the shore provided shellfish and seabird. As these supplies waxed and waned, so the group moved from site to site. Such communities may have continued their predatory way of life well beyond the time when the first farmers began to make their way from the Continent to the shores of Britain. Some already possessed the domesticated dog and had begun to exert an influence upon the countryside deliberately or indirectly by fire and interference with the natural tree cover. Some like the Irish Larnian had seen advantage in polishing stone and were already using the polished stone axe. But future developments lay not with these communities but with the new colonists arriving from overseas.

The first farmers

By 3500 bc the number of new colonists gaining the shores of Britain had reached a sufficient size to leave an unmistakable trace upon the archaeological record. Their coming was probably in itself unremarkable – family groups in small boats arriving intermittently over a spread of years – but it marks nonetheless a major watershed in our history for the new immigrants brought with them livestock and seed-corn and a well established knowledge of subsistence farming. All developments henceforth are built upon the potential that food production within the control of man could underwrite.

Colonisation must have been an exciting affair, though one probably beset by relatively few problems. The old native population of hunter-gatherers had remained relatively small and would have posed few threats.

Indeed little evidence survives of actual contacts between immigrant and native, though some mutually beneficial exchanges may well have occurred from time to time. Britain would have offered the colonists many of the basic ingredients such pioneers would have sought – ample room for expansion, a rich woodland readily tamed by the implements already within the farmers' tool kit and a natural fertility that only virgin land can offer. The woods too contained a range of animals soon to be put to good use, notably pig, red and roe deer, to be followed in later centuries by the horse. Actual landfall may well have owed as much to the vagaries of wind and current as to intention for early farming sites are found widely scattered around the British Isles.

Over the next centuries the farmers established themselves, grew in numbers and spread leaving a trail of woodland clearance to mark their presence. They appear to have remained in family groups, at first favouring the individual homestead rather than settled village life. Where traces of houses have survived these are small and roughly rectangular, timber-framed with walls made of turf or wattle-and-daub, no doubt surmounted by a thatched or turfed roof. The surviving implements that the farmers possessed may look crude to modern eyes but we must never forget that these were employed by those well-versed in their use backed by the collective experience of many centuries. Stone and flint figure prominently for heavy duty tasks. For grinding corn the saddle quern was used. Timber felling and shaping required a range of axes, 8 adzes and chisels. Lighter domestic chores like skin preparation were achieved with scrapers, 9 knives and borers; while for hunting and protection the farmers developed a range of leaf-shaped projectile points. A variety of bones as well as antler continued to provide material for other tools. The antler pick now 10 became a tool of major importance especially

8 Axeheads of flint and stone. (bottom) A flint axe in course of manufacture: a block roughly worked to shape, prepared to final shape by flaking, end product ground to cutting edge and polished. (top) Roughed-out block of stone and finished axe.

on the chalk lands of the south and east where it served both as hoe and quarrying tool. Bones were cut and polished down to form borers, pins and coarse needles as well as beads for personal adornment. But the axe was the implement which had overriding significance for these early settlers and while many of the raw materials for everyday implements would have lain ready to hand, certain sources of fine-grained stone and flint for axe production were particularly sought out – Langdale, Tievebulliagh, Craig Llwyd and Cornwall for stone; the Sussex chalk lands for flint. Most stone sources could be worked as outcrops with the need for only minor delvings into the parent rock but for best quality unweathered flint, the farmers had to mine. Axes made from these sources were traded and exchanged over long distances and it is not difficult to perceive how the axe itself could have become a symbol of their struggle against the external world and an object of value and veneration in its own right. How else are we to explain axes made of jadeite, ground and polished with 11 infinite labour to such a thinness that the question of normal functional use cannot be entertained? The farmers too had brought with them a knowledge of pottery-making. The pots were initially simple, aimed more at serving basic needs than delighting the eye. Round-based bowls and deeper storage vessels 12 were made in a dark brown often gritty fabric and given a plain smoothed surface. When decoration was applied, in the form of scored lines or simple impressions pushed into the clay when leather-hard, this was quite restrained.

What of course are absent from this list are the softer organic substances – wood, skin, rope and reed which survive only rarely in the British Isles and then only in waterlogged conditions. Yet surrounded by woodlands and forest it would be absurd to suppose that wood did not play a major if not dominant role in the

10 *right.* Pick made from the antler of a red deer. The bez and trez tines have been cut away as well as the crown, leaving the brow tine to form the pick. Length 22.5 in (56.5 cm)

11 *left.* Axe of polished jadeite, probably found near Canterbury, Kent. Length 8.6 in (21.9 cm). The axe is in a pristine state and was clearly not intended for normal use. The rock from which it was made probably comes from the Alpine region.

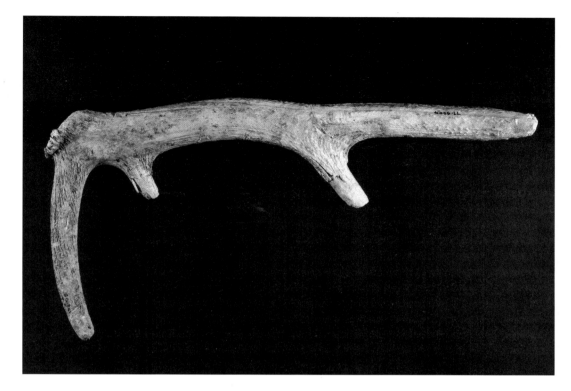

12 *right.* A range of pottery bowls from the first farming period (left to right) from Etton, Cambridgeshire, Heslerton, N. Yorkshire, Staines, Surrey and Clacton, Essex. Diam. of Heslerton bowl 10.5 in (26.7 cm)

9 *left.* Other elements of the Early Farmers' flint tool kit: (top row) laurel leaf point, two leaf-shaped arrowheads and an awl; (bottom row) flake knives and scrapers. Length of laurel leaf 3.75 ins (9.5 cm)

life of the early settlers. Work in the peat deposits of the Somerset Levels has shown that by this time man was not only skilled in the selection of wood for specific purposes but had already embarked in certain areas upon active management of the woodlands as a useful 13 resource. Surviving relics from the period remain rare but remains of wooden hafts for axes from Etton in the Cambridgeshire Fens and Ehenside Tarn in Cumbria show man selecting appropriately resilient woods (ash and beech) and being capable of producing from them a well-balanced hatchet. A broad 14 bladed object also from Ehenside Tarn was probably a digging paddle extending the range of agricultural implements to a form which could not have been produced in any other material at this time. The long bow from Meare (see inside back cover) made of yew, demonstrates a formidable defensive/offensive capability for, when teamed with a long-shafted arrow tipped with flint, this weapon would have had an effective range of at least sixty metres. Such survivals offer mere glimpses of a total range of implement and use which we must infer as best we can from other evidence. The light plough itself is well attested, not from surviving specimens but from the less perishable traces of cross-ploughing preserved beneath the mound of the Long Barrow at South Street in Wiltshire. The traces, cut into the top of the underlying chalk rock, themselves imply powerful traction and with it no doubt yoke and harness, whether for man or beast.

13 The Walton Heath hurdle track, Somerset Levels. The track, a late example, was made of hurdles dumped and positioned in the marsh about 2300 bc to help movement across the wet land. The hurdles were woven from hazel rods taken from a coppiced woodland on the nearby Polden Hills.

14 Stone hatchet and wooden digging paddle from Ehenside Tarn, Cumbria. The flaked and ground axehead is made from rock obtained in Langdale. The haft is made of beech wood. Length of paddle is 20.1 in (51.0 cm)

Enclosures, tombs and shrines

It was not long, however, before the farmers embarked upon tasks which were to leave a lasting mark upon the countryside of Britain. In the south and east a variety of more-or-less circular enclosures were built. These vary in size but all were constructed by throwing up one or more circular banks of earth and stone quarried from discontinuous 'causewayed' ditches. On excavation these sites often show evidence of communal feasting and many must have served as points where the scattered population could foregather, for the need to meet would soon have become a necessity to arrange marriages, to exchange commodities and gifts and to establish or reaffirm those obligations and loyalties which form the very structure of human society. No doubt other enclosures served different needs. That on Hambledon Hill, Dorset was large enough to embrace not only settlement but sources of flint, pasturage for animals and perhaps even a small acreage of cereal crop. But here a circular area defined by its own bank and discontinuous ditch had also been set aside for the dead. In this bodies were laid in shallow pits until such time as the flesh had decayed before the bones were collected and re-used in further complex rituals. Most of the bone residue was laid carefully in heaps within the ditches but certain bones, in particular many skulls, had been set aside and placed separately along the ditch floor. It is highly probable that in such acts we can see an appeal to the power of the dead and more particularly to the power of the ancestors, for the need to stress lineal descent to preserve land use and tenure could well have imbued the family ancestors with great power and prestige. Whatever the precise form these

beliefs may have taken, a respect for, and a manipulation of, the dead is a recurrent theme amongst the surviving ritual monuments of the period.

Just how much time and effort the farmers were prepared to devote towards the construction of monuments to the dead is shown by the surviving long barrows and cairns of southern Britain and the massive stone chambered tombs of the north and west. In southern and eastern England, mounds measuring up to 120 metres long, of earth and chalk quarried from flanking ditches were heaped over the mortuaries to which the bodies of the dead had first been brought. Only rarely in lowland Britain and mostly in Yorkshire was cremation practised at this time. In such a tomb once the mound had been erected no further burials could be added. The stone-built tombs of the north and west show a much greater range of practice and many on examination reveal a history of alteration and addition over time. In and around the Cotswolds stone mortuary chambers were constructed, later to be incorporated into the sides or widest (eastern) end of huge trapezoidal cairns of stone, framed by drystone walling. In Wales, the simple dolmen formed by four large upright slabs supporting a massive capstone, was similarly used and covered by a mound. Yet another form of long cairn was built along the raised beaches and rich coastal soils of west and south-west Scotland. In these the stone-built chamber was often sub-divided into segments by low transverse slabs. More elaborate still are the Court Cairns of north-western Ireland especially common in the Counties of Leitrim, Sligo and Mayo, which take their name from the elaborate 'forecourt' built in front of the chamber's entrance.

In different areas tombs saw differing use. In the Cotswolds the chambers and passages which led to them allowed access for successive burials until a final 'blocking' brought this practice to an end. Many on examination have revealed the bones of earlier burials pushed aside and stacked to make room for later interments, and this too is a feature of the south-west Scottish tombs though in these cremated burials are also known. As for the Court Cairns of northern Ireland, few burials survive but there is more than a hint that some were removed from the chambers to be buried in the forecourts where small amounts of cremated bone mixed with sherds of pottery, charcoal and animal bones have frequently been recovered. Such monuments show how very varied could be the ritual concerned with death. Yet certain features do recur. Though the structures themselves are often impressive and represent a massive outlay in both time and labour, few objects were placed with the body, emphasis being placed upon the family or community rather than upon the individual. In many cairns evidence of co-operative effort can be seen in the way that sections of the mound have been constructed separately suggesting, as do the segmented 'causewayed' quarry ditches of the enclosures, work by groups of people working towards a common end but intent upon preserving evidence of their separate contributions. In many tombs too where bodies had been interred certain bones are frequently under-represented. Often these are the skull and long bones, suggesting again the deliberate removal of ancestral relics, and it is precisely these bones which recur in the enclosures in non-funerary contexts. Of the tombs of the north and west some, particularly the Court Cairns, seem to have served more as shrines than as tombs and may thus have provided a focus for the community similar to that of many of the enclosures of the south.

The amount of labour involved in erecting tomb and enclosure was considerable. Together these monuments stand testimony both to the effectiveness of the farming, which must now have been capable of producing a considerable surplus to allow so much labour to be devoted to tasks other than food production, and to the ability of the farmers to undertake large-scale communal tasks. But by the middle of the millennium there are signs that the structure of society was changing. As the farming community had expanded, its need to establish rights to herds and land use must have begun to press. That these rights had on occasion to be defended is shown by the massive defences constructed round the Hambledon Hill enclosure and at sites like Crickley Hill in Gloucestershire and Carn Brea in Cornwall. At Hambledon the scale of these defences is quite astonishing. An entire hill with attendant spurs was defended by a ditch and timber-framed rampart system enclosing an area of some 160 acres. At Crickley Hill the density of arrowheads recovered from around the entrance shot towards the defenders provides vivid evidence of actual hostilities as does the destruction of part of the ramparts at Hambledon by fire and the discovery of a young man lying by the central gate with an arrow lodged in his chest. If land had to be given up and rights defended, perhaps surrendered, belief in the power of the ancestors may have been shaken and eventually undermined to be replaced by the visibly more obvious power of the living.

An age of great ceremony

During the second half of the third millennium a much greater diversity in pottery and implement begins to appear. Heavily ornamented necked bowls in the Peterborough tradition are soon in widespread use over England and Wales, at first retaining the round base, later to appear in flat based forms. Other comparable but more restricted styles emerge in north-eastern England, in Scotland and in Ireland. For the first time cord and thread are used extensively to decorate the surface – a timely reminder of their elsewhere unseen presence. Contemporary are the flat-based bowls and large storage vessels of the Grooved Ware tradition found from Cornwall to the Orkneys, from Ireland to Essex. Often highly

15

16

17

18

15 Peterborough Ware bowl of 'Mortlake style' from Hedsor, Buckinghamshire decorated with twisted cord impressions. Diam. of bowl 6.9 in (17.5 cm)

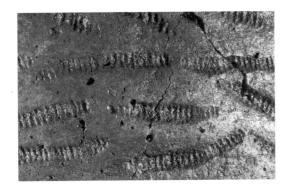

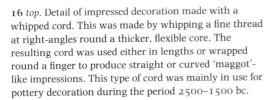

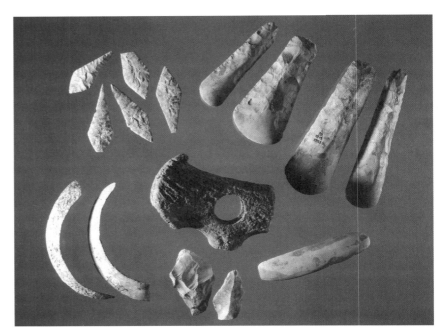

16 *top*. Detail of impressed decoration made with a whipped cord. This was made by whipping a fine thread at right-angles round a thicker, flexible core. The resulting cord was used either in lengths or wrapped round a finger to produce straight or curved 'maggot'-like impressions. This type of cord was mainly in use for pottery decoration during the period 2500–1500 bc.

17 *above*. Detail of impressed decoration made with a two-strand twisted cord. This type of cord was particularly favoured for decorating pottery during the period 2500–1000 bc.

18 *above right*. Groove Ware vessel from the enclosure at Durrington Walls, Wiltshire. The division of the decoration into vertical panels is typical of the Durrington Walls style. Height of vessel 5.75 in (14.5 cm)

19 *right*. A group of 3 flint axes, a flint adze, 5 lozenge-shaped flint arrowheads, a polished flint knife, 2 flint flakes, an antler 'macehead' and 2 boar-tusk blades, found probably with a burial, in a pit dug into the top of a Round Cairn at Ayton East Field, N. Yorkshire. Length of longest axe 5.3 in (13.5 cm)

decorated these vessels frequently carried incised or grooved ornament coupled with strips of clay applied so as to break the surface of the vessel into panels and form further decorative motifs. Changes too occur in the tools and weapons of the period. Waisted axes, discoidal, plano-convex and polished edged knives were now produced. Chisel-ended asymmetric and lozenge-shaped arrowheads join the leaf-shaped forms already in use. Tools made from boars' tusks and antler and stone maceheads also appear. Some show considerable skill in their execution and embody an outlay in time not to be equated with functional advantage. Many of these are therefore items likely to have been prized within the community at large and signal a change towards a more ranked society in which the fine became available to the few.

In some areas, principally in eastern Ireland and northern Scotland, new forms of chambered tomb were being built. The largest of these were monuments of colossal proportions. At Knowth in the Boyne Valley a great circular mound of earth, turf and stone up to ninety metres in diameter had been heaped eleven metres high over two stone-built tombs, one with a single chamber, the other cruciform in plan. One tomb was entered from the west, the other from the east each by way of a lengthy passage, the longer measuring thirty metres. The mound itself was bounded by massive kerbstones richly decorated with 'megalithic art' and many of the stones used in the construction of the tombs are similarly decorated, as were those at the comparable nearby tomb of New Grange. In the finer chambers *corbelling* was used to span the roof, a technique taken to near perfection in the tomb of Maes Howe on Orkney. Yet the contents of these tombs bear little relationship to their size or to the labour involved in their erection. Cremation was the rite in Ireland, the bones sometimes placed on stone basins which

can themselves be decorated. But of objects placed regularly with the dead only coarse stab-and-drag decorated pottery, bone and antler pins and a few small pendants survive. In Orkney where both inhumation and cremation was practised the grave goods are more numerous but hardly spectacular. Stone maceheads, a series of strange knobbed and spiked objects of a type similar to others found within the contemporary settlements and as stray finds, occur along with pottery of the northern styles and animal bones, often in some numbers. Clearly in these tombs communal effort and communal ritual were still of paramount importance rather than the status of the individual, but there are also hints of

20 Megalithic art on the underside of the roof-stone of the east chamber at New Grange, Co. Meath.

more sophisticated thoughts. At New Grange a slot had been constructed above the entrance to the passage. The tomb itself had been erected so that for a few days either side of the winter solstice, the sun's light shone through this slot along the length of the passage to illuminate the chamber. Even today for those who have witnessed this event, the effect is breathtaking. Many of these elaborate structures must, like the Court Cairns, have functioned as far more than simple tombs, and the rituals performed may well have played a central role in the life of the communities they served.

Other forms of ritual defy interpretation. Tombs of the Clava group in north-east Scotland often incorporate 'cup-marked' stones and many a rock face in the uplands of Northumberland, west Yorkshire and west Scotland carries 'cup-and-ring' or more complex designs pecked into its surface. Their significance remains unexplained. Other structures too were being built now in the partially cleared landscape whose function appears primarily ceremonial and sometimes clearly linked with observations of the sun, less often with the moon. Henge monuments – circular enclosures formed usually by continuous ditch and external bank broken by one, or more often two, opposed entrances were constructed over much of south-eastern Britain. Some, like the first enclosure at Stonehenge, were aligned upon a phase of the sun – here the mid-summer sunrise – implying not only solar observation but also recognition of regular events and through them the measurement of time. In the north and west, stone circles began to bristle on the upland slopes, some small but others like the Ring of Brodgar a major feature of the landscape. More enigmatic monuments, such as Silbury Hill, the largest man-made mound in Europe, 40 metres high and 165 metres across containing a quarter of a million cubic metres of

quarried chalk, or the parallel banked 'cursus' give less clue as to their function. Like Silbury, the Dorset Cursus, in its final form an earthwork traversing almost ten kilometres of southern downland, was not a labour to be undertaken lightly but little survives to offer real insight into the reason for its existence.

Around 2000 bc a new series of major enclosures were built in central southern England at Durrington, Marden and Avebury in Wiltshire (the last incorporating a massive stone circle) and Knowlton and Mount Pleasant in Dorset. Those at Durrington Walls near Amesbury and Mount Pleasant outside Dorchester preserve the remains of large circular public buildings, framed with massive timbers, erected within them. The ditch alone at Durrington may have required 40,000 man days to excavate.

Yet the complexity of thought and engineering skill that many of these monuments imply is hardly reflected in the implements which made them. The stone hatchet and the antler pick remain the prime tools for felling and shaping timber and for delving and quarrying at least the chalk rocks of southern and eastern England. What could be achieved with these implements is shown not only by the

22

21 Three carved stone balls from Old Deer, Aberdeenshire and Rossshire. Nearly 400 balls are known, almost all about 2.75 in (7 cm) in diam. Those with six projecting knobs, either plain or decorated, are the most common. Practically confined to Scotland, being particularly common in the north east between the Tay and the Moray Firth, nearly all are stray finds, but similar balls have been found in the village at Skara Brae. Their use and significance remain unknown.

22 Rock-outcrop at Kilmichael Glassary, Argyll showing typical array of cup and cup-and-ring engravings.

23 View looking into the cleared galleries of pit 15 of the Grimes Graves Flint Mines, in Norfolk. The flint seam known as the 'floor-stone' can be clearly seen at the base of the chalk pillars.

24 The Grimes Graves 'Goddess'. A crude representation of the female form carved in chalk. Found in 1939 at the base of the shaft of Pit 15, one of the flint-mines at Grimes Graves, Norfolk. Height 4.05 in (10.3 cm)

raw material was worked on site down to the stage of implements roughly trimmed to shape 8 but much must have been transported in the form of unworked blocks to be fashioned elsewhere as time and need dictated. Those who mined and worked the flint at Grimes Graves used Grooved Ware as did those who erected the great enclosures of southern Britain. Exceptionally at Grimes Graves they left behind a crude representation in chalk of a human figure – 'the Goddess'. One of the great 24 curiosities of British prehistory is why so little naturalistic art survives. The goddess along with the wooden god-dolly from the Somerset Levels, and fragments of other chalk-cut figures from Windmill Hill, Maiden Castle and elsewhere are all that survive, beside simple phalli, of three dimensional forms, and all are fashioned with such crudity as to suggest that a strong taboo prevailed over accurate human representation. This feeling is heightened by other carved objects which hint at a face but never express it explicitly – the eyebrow-and-eye motifs of Megalithic art or the exquisite flint macehead found recently at 25

rock hewn ditches of the great enclosures but also by the massive flint-mine complex at Grimes Graves, near Brandon in Norfolk.

The mining of flint at Grimes Graves was at its peak around 2100–1800 bc. Flint occurred in three separate bands in the chalk and all were utilised, but the deepest was the best – the floor-stone. Unweathered, below the destructive action of periglacial frost, the floor-stone lay in large tabular lumps. To reach it the miners were prepared to sink shafts up to fifteen metres deep, and having reached it to exploit the layer by digging radial galleries out 23 from the base of the shaft. A rough calculation indicates that one of these galleried mines could yield as much as forty tonnes of floor-stone giving a figure in excess of 14,000 tonnes for the entire site, enough to make twenty-eight million implements. Some of this

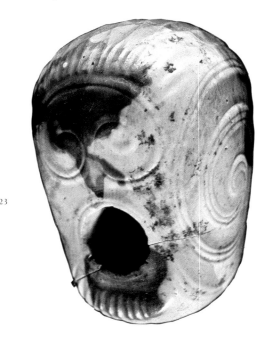

26 Stone-built shelves and cupboards inside one of the huts at Skara Brae, Orkney. On the floor can be seen a quern and a stone slab-lined box.

25 Flint macehead found in the eastern tomb beneath the great mound at Knowth, Co. Meath. It lay between the jamb stones at the entrance to the right-hand chamber. The flint has been shaped and decorated by grinding and polishing.
3.1 × 2.1 in (8 × 5.4 cm)

Knowth. We are thus prevented from glimpsing our early farmers as they would have seen themselves even at one remove. Skeletal evidence suggests a range of stature but with an average of 1.6 metres. Of clothing nothing survives but with the absence of any evidence for weaving we must suppose that garments made of sewn skins remained the usual form of dress.

Our best glimpse of domestic life survives not from the mainland but from Orkney, from the villages of Skara Brae and Rinyo. Some allowance must be made for the setting – on the windswept edge of the northern isles – and there is no need to assume that villages in climatically more favoured areas would have needed to huddle quite so compactly but equally there is no reason to suppose that in its general layout a timber and turf house in the south would have differed greatly. Here in Orkney, we find fashioned in stone within the houses, the bed boxes, shelves and storage compartments, which elsewhere do not survive – a rare but priceless insight into homes of four thousand years ago.

The arrival of copper and Beaker pottery

By 2000 bc other and more far reaching events were also taking shape. A knowledge of copper-working had been introduced and new influences to affect other spheres of life were coming from the Continent. Though knowledge of metallurgy had reached the British Isles relatively late compared to other parts of Continental Europe, once established the new metal smiths pursued their craft with vigour. The availability of copper deposits, principally in south-western Ireland, but also in western Scotland, north Wales, Devon and Cornwall was a tremendous boon and made the new industries springing up virtually self-sufficient. At first ores possessing arsenical impurities were particularly favoured as this natural alloy gave the implements a hardness greater than that of pure copper.

Other new and influential immigrants began to make their presence felt. Whatever the skills or knowledge were that they brought with them, both they and the new type of pottery which they introduced quickly gained acceptance amongst the native communities. This new Beaker pottery is very different from 27 what had gone before. It is well made, thin-

27 A range of Beaker pottery (from the left) from Hemp Knoll, Bishops Cannings, Wiltshire; Rudstone, Humberside; Goodmanham, Humberside; Lambourn, Berkshire and Hitchin, Hertfordshire.

walled and fired under controlled conditions often to give a handsome rich, reddish-brown surface. The earliest carry the imprint of a fine twisted cord wound round the vessel from top to bottom or narrow horizontal zones of impressed lines made with a rectangular toothed comb stamp. Great care was often 28 lavished upon the decoration of the finest vessels, the geometric patterns being set with great precision in evenly spaced bands around the pot. Many Beakers embody a marvellous sense of symmetry and some exploit the ambiguity which arises naturally when blank and patterned spaces are opposed. Both events served to fuel and underline the social changes now in train. For the first time a greater emphasis on personal wealth becomes a prominent feature of the archaeological record, at least in death. Occasionally burials had already appeared accompanied by rare or finely worked artefacts sometimes set beneath a round mound of earth. Such burials now become far more common. A Beaker was the most frequent object to be placed with the body but some of the first metal goods to circulate in Britain – simple copper tanged and 29

28 *above*. Detail of impressed decoration made with a toothed 'comb'. The 'comb', made by shaping rectangular, or less often pointed, teeth on the edge of a rib-bone is the most characteristic technique employed by potters making Beaker pottery. A similar comb was also employed to decorate some Food Vessels. It remained in use from about 2100 bc to about 1500 bc.

29 *above left*. Objects accompanying the body in a grave beneath a round earthen mound at Barnack, Cambridgeshire. These comprised a fine pottery Beaker decorated with patterns made with a rectangular toothed comb, a stone wristguard with gold rivet caps, a bone pendant or toggle and a small tanged metal knife blade. Height of Beaker 9.5 in (24 cm)

30 *left*. Decorated sheet gold disc found at Kilmuckridge, Co. Wexford. Gold discs are an insular adaptation in gold of the ornamental heads of Central European bronze 'racquet-headed' pins. The disc was attached by thread through the two central holes and some show evidence of stitching also round the edge. Diam. 2.8 in (7.1 cm)

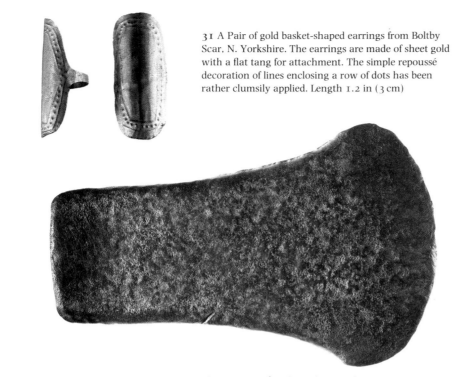

31 A Pair of gold basket-shaped earrings from Boltby Scar, N. Yorkshire. The earrings are made of sheet gold with a flat tang for attachment. The simple repoussé decoration of lines enclosing a row of dots has been rather clumsily applied. Length 1.2 in (3 cm)

32 Thick butted copper axehead of early type. Length 5.85 in (15.1 cm)

33 Bronze halberd blade from Kells, Co. Meath. The blade was attached more or less at right-angles to a wooden haft by means of rivets which unlike those on the contemporary daggers are often arranged asymetrically. Length of blade 9.75 in (24.7 cm)

riveted knives, awls and razors can also now be found with the dead and more rarely objects of precious metal – gold decorated discs and 30 basket-shaped earrings. Flint arrowheads of 31 the barbed and tanged variety and stone wristguards (worn on the inside of the wrist to protect the archer from the return of the bow string) show the importance of the bowman, while v-perforated buttons and pendants reveal something of current tastes in personal adornment. The tombs of the dead are less spectacular than before but more numerous. Successive collective burial was abandoned in favour of individual interment though graves were often grouped in cemeteries or made successively in the same shaft or mound. Many are simple pits back-filled and probably once enhanced by a grave marker of wood or stone, though these rarely survive. In the north, the body may be protected by stone slabs set to form a simple box or cist and on rare occasions elsewhere traces of a wooden coffin may survive. The majority however, were interred simply, beneath or in-set into a round mound of earth or stone.

It would be wrong to give the impression, however, that what was deemed appropriate to place with the dead must reflect directly the lives and conditions of the living. Funeral rites are governed by rules based upon beliefs and without knowing the precise nature of those beliefs the actual choice of object may well mislead. The thick-butted flat copper axeheads 32 for example, one of the first copper products made in Britain, were never placed with the dead nor were the halberds made by the Irish 33 coppersmiths. In fact throughout the period

34 Gold lunula from Blessington, Co. Wicklow of 'classical' type, a group distinguished not only by their thinness and width but also by the precision of their ornamentation. Overall width 8.65 in (22 cm)

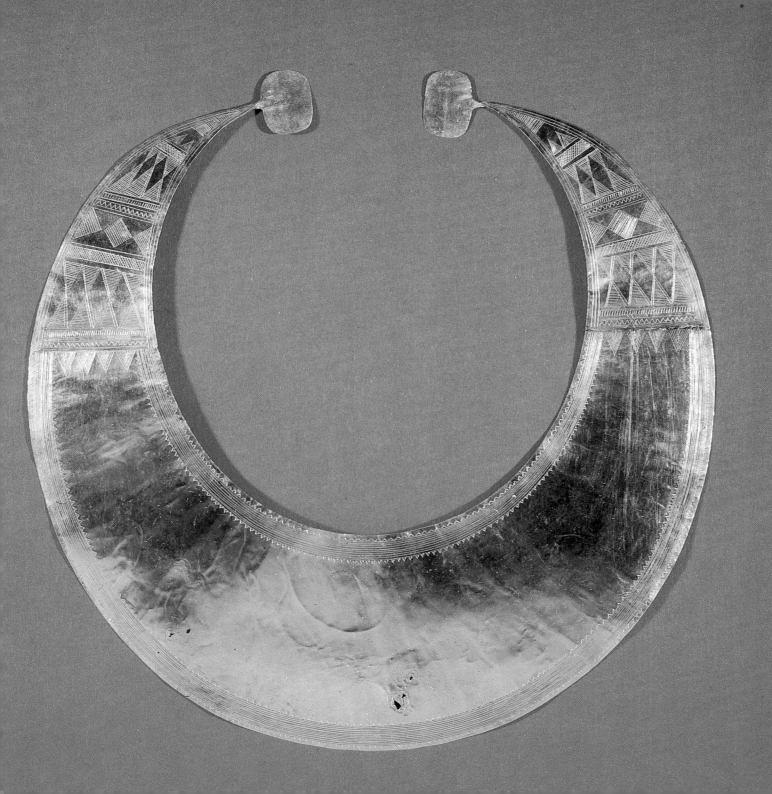

when copper and later bronze implements and weaponry were to be in current use only a restricted range ever reached the grave. Nor were all objects of prestige considered appropriate. The gold concentric neck ornaments known as *lunulae* have been found only as 34 isolated finds or in hoards, yet these must surely have been greatly prized by the living. Made of gold beaten out into sheet and cut to shape, the finest carry carefully engraved

geometric patterns drawing on a repertoire similar to, but somewhat different from, those used by the Beaker potters. Perhaps their value was too great to be 'lost' in the grave.

From the same period come three of the most extraordinary objects to be found in Prehistoric Britain, the Folkton Drums. Made 35 of chalk and varying in size from 10.4 to 14.6 centimetres in diameter, the drums have been carefully carved around the sides and top. On

35 The Folkton Drums. Three carved cylinders of chalk. In addition to the eyebrow-and-eye motifs each carries panelled geometric designs round the side. The top of the smallest cylinder is decorated with a pair of circles surrounded at first by concentric circles then

by concentric opposed arcs. The top of the largest carries a 4-rayed star pattern with concentric circles at the centre, and the third, a group of four concentric circles. Diam. of largest drum is 5.85 in (14.8 cm)

each the sides have been divided into four panels, two broad and two narrow. On two an eyebrow-and-eye motif has been worked, one incised, the other in relief, reminiscent of Megalithic art. Other elements of their design copy Grooved Ware patterns. These objects are unique yet in their shape and in the way that their decoration has been created, in part by chip carving, lies a suggestion that similar objects may well once have existed in wood. In

terms of time expended in their making, the Folkton Drums must have been highly valued yet they had been placed with the burial of a child in one of a number of simple graves beneath an equally unremarkable mound of earth, with no other obvious signs of distinction. For the archaeologist such a find offers insufficient clues for its comprehension.

Bronze and the rise of the Wessex élite

Objects of copper were gradually replaced by new forms made in the more durable alloy, tin-bronze. The ready availability of tin in south-western Britain and perhaps in smaller more localised deposits in Scotland and Ireland enabled the transition to bronze-working to be swift and without the hesitancy which sometimes marks this phase elsewhere in Europe. A mix comprising 10% tin and 90% copper yields the best results and this alloy was quickly standardised. Once adopted the bronzesmiths appear for a period to have developed their own ideas uninfluenced by Continental fashion. Insular forms of halberd and flat riveted knives appear, while axeheads in particular take on a more elegant appearance showing refinements in the way of flanges and stop-ridge, pointing to the adoption of the elbowed split haft in replacement of the straight haft. Not all the implements were plain. Axes were often ornamented with punched decoration, like three of the axes from a hoard of four recovered from a round barrow on Willerby Wold, Yorkshire. Embossing too was a technique now in use, first employed on sheet metal bracelets in the north.

A change to a less egalitarian society seems not to have occurred without tension and major change in ritual and belief. Around 1700 bc a massive wooden defensive palisade was constructed at Mount Pleasant within the existing earthwork enclosure, but was soon destroyed. Inside a setting of sarsen stones was erected to mark the site of the former timber building. A similar transformation from wood to stone took place at the Sanctuary on Overton Hill, while at Stonehenge, the erection of a double circle of blue stones had been commenced. This work never saw completion for the scheme was overtaken by a yet more grandiose conception culminating in the massive sarsen monument whose tumbled remains we see today. This was to be a monument unique in Europe – an outer circle of thirty mighty sarsen blocks, each nearly four metres high capped with lintels set around a still more massive horseshoe setting of five free-standing trilithons. Each stone was laboriously dressed to shape but significantly, and perhaps symbolically, the stones had been joined one to another by techniques more familiar in carpentry than in masonry using tongue-and-groove and mortise-and-tenon joints. The blue stones too were re-worked and rearranged more than once till finally placed in position as they are today – a free-standing circle set between the sarsen ring and the trilithons, with a further blue stone horseshoe setting placed at the centre of the monument. Such an undertaking would have required an immense outlay of time and labour. The sarsen blocks, weighing anything up to fifty tons apiece, must each have been hauled from the Marlborough Downs, a distance of some

36 Group of four bronze axeheads, three decorated, one plain, with low cast flanges and incipient stop-ridges, deposited together during the erection of a round barrow on Willerby Wold, Humberside. Longest axehead 7.3 in (18.6 cm)

37 'Mortise and tenon' on standing sarsen upright and fallen lintel at Stonehenge.

twenty-five miles. Transporting, shaping, jointing and erecting these stones would have required upwards of three million working man days. Not only was this a formidable feat of engineering but the whole enterprise would have called for sustained and firm direction, leaving little doubt in our minds that the social structure that had now come into being possessed at its head a new and overriding authority. Yet in the marking of sites of former timber structures and in the very techniques used to build Stonehenge we can see a positive move to placate by honouring and preserving something of the past even in the midst of change.

The area round Stonehenge became the focus for monuments raised in honour of the dead. Round barrows of many forms made of 38

quarried chalk or scraped-up earth cluster conspicuously along the slopes of the Downs often forming cemeteries of imposing size. Amidst these barrows the upper echelons of this new society now emerge in the archaeological record. For it became the practice, at least in Wessex and for a limited period, to place much of their acquired wealth with the dead. Renewed contacts with the Continent had introduced a taste for new fashions. As in other areas of western and northern Europe, the prestige weapon becomes the bronze dagger, sometimes given an elaborate hilt and pommel, though in Britain these and the sheaths in which they had once been carried were usually of organic materials and seldom survive. Rare commodities were also sought like jet and amber from the shores of the North Sea, shale from Dorset, Irish gold and manmade faience. Much of this for a time now reached the grave.

The earlier graves tend to be the richest. The body of the man laid out upon the surface of the ground beneath Bush Barrow in the parish of Wilsford in Wiltshire had three daggers placed near to his right hand. Two (the third could not be recovered) were of triangular form, one of copper, one of bronze and both bear traces of their former sheaths once made of wood with a leather lining. The hilt of the copper dagger had also been of wood and carried a chevron pattern made with minute pins of gold. Also of bronze was a flanged axehead interred with its haft near the head and wrapped in cloth, for traces of this still survive in corrosion on its blade. On his chest lay a lozenge-shaped plaque, perforated at 39 opposed corners for attachment, of which only the gold facing plate survives. A design in the form of concentric lozenges has been finely traced into its surface, the centre filled with cross-hatching, the outer zone with chevrons. Near the daggers lay a similar decorated plate for a belt attachment and a smaller lozenge in

sheet gold. With these had been placed other items suggestive of high status: beside the right arm a mace of which the polished head, made from fossiliferous limestone, survived though not its wooden shaft, and a baton, also of wood, though only the decorated bone mounts, cut to a dog-tooth pattern, remained. The daggers from this grave with their triangular shape and six slender rivets by which the hilt had been attached closely resemble contemporary weapons in Brittany and speak of close contacts across the Channel. Other objects show ideas received from further afield. Small pendants in the form of metal-hilted halberds, from graves at Preshute and Wilsford, copy forms current not in the West but in Central Europe and a pendant shaped like a metal ingot must have been similarly inspired. Discs of amber, bound around the edge with gold resemble others found not in Western or Central Europe but in the east Mediterranean. Such items are important for they illustrate over what distances ideas and sometimes even objects were being transmitted. Amongst other items from these early graves come small pottery cups with pimpled surface, multi-strand necklaces of amber beads, the strands separated by complex-bored space-

39 Gold coverings for a belt-hook and lozenge-shaped decorations found with a male skeleton in Bush Barrow, Wilsford, Wiltshire, the richest of the earlier Wessex graves. Length of largest lozenge 7.3 in (18.6 cm)

38 Aerial photograph of the Stonehenge region showing the Normanton Group of round barrows in the foreground. Stonehenge itself can be seen beyond the road leading from the bottom of the picture.

40 Cup and cover from Aldbourne, Wiltshire. The use of dot filling for decoration is very like that on the Melfort jet necklace (50) This type of cup is not common and is found only with later Wessex burials. Diam. of cup 4 in (10.2 cm)

plates in the same material, cone-shaped pendants covered in sheet gold and finely decorated, battleaxes of stone and, from Clandon, Dorset, a mace-head of jet with inset studs of gold. An air of wealth and ostentation hangs heavy about these graves.

Later graves lack gold and many of the items can be found on occasion in graves well beyond the confines of Wessex. Nowhere else, however, do we find so great a concentration. In these the rite is cremation occasionally contained in a pottery urn or accompanied by a small cup of Aldbourne type. Daggers from 40 these graves are ogival, the product of insular thought and development and if anything more imposing than those from the earlier graves. Cast grooves follow the edge of the weapon and the blade can be further enhanced with pounced decoration. Perforated 41 whetstones and finely carved bone 'tweezers' are other items often found. From abroad came a taste for other trinkets. Bronze pins, often copied locally in bone, show continued contact with Central Europe and beads of faience were now particularly favoured, strung in quantity or mixed with other beads of amber, shale and jet. Though the technique of making faience was now known in Britain, its origins lie again around the shores of the East Mediterranean.

Elsewhere the population had less access to wealth or chose to keep it with the living following their own beliefs, for graves with prestige objects are relatively rare. Yet exceptionally such graves can rival the best in Wessex. At Hove on the coast of Sussex an oak coffin contained the remains of a body with which had been placed a stone battleaxe, whetstone, bronze dagger and decorated handled cup carved from a single lump of amber. At Rillaton in Cornwall the body of a 42 man was accompanied by beads, a fine bronze dagger and a unique handled cup of gold, whose corrugated surface and shape recall the

44 Grooved bronze dagger of later Wessex type, bronze spearhead, bronze pin and stone battleaxe found with a skeleton in a stone cist at Snowshill, Gloucestershire. The bronze pin is similar to others found in Bohemia. The spearhead is particularly interesting as it combines both tang and cast socket to aid attachment. Length of dagger 8.7 in (22.1 cm)

41 Detail of the blade of a bronze dagger of later Wessex type from Rillaton, Cornwall, showing grooves and pounced decoration.

42 The Rillaton gold cup found in 1837 with a skeleton in a stone cist beneath a round cairn of stones. A grooved bronze dagger (**41**) and beads accompanied the body. The body of the cup was beaten out from a single piece of gold. The handle, made from a second piece, was attached by rivets with lozenge-shaped washers. Height 3.3 in (8.3 cm)

Beaker pottery still in use. But perhaps the most spectacular of all objects which have survived from this period comes from north Wales – the splendid cape of beaten gold found in a grave at Mold in Flintshire. The embossed decoration of this piece conveys the idea of multiple strands of beads while the rows of holes which follow the upper and lower edges of the cape show how the gold once was attached to an inner organic lining presumably of leather.

For a full knowledge of the range of bronze tools and weapons belonging to this phase we must look beyond the graves to stray finds and hoards. From these we can gather that the spear was in use tipped with a formidable tanged blade or one with a cast hollow socket. The development of the cast socket was a major technical advance demanding a complex three-piece mould and was to become the standard technique for hafting not only a wide range of spearheads but eventually the bulk of the everyday tools in use over the next millennium. The willingness of the bronzesmith to experiment with hafting techniques is well illustrated by the curious spearhead from Snowshill in Gloucestershire where tang and socket have been wrought on the same implement. Thick lugged chisels and thin bladed oval razors were other implements now in use.

43 Gold Cape from Mold, Flintshire (Clwyd). The cape was found in 1833 around the bones of a skeleton contained in a stone cist beneath a round mound of earth and stone. The cape is made from a single sheet of gold and is covered in repoussé ornament. This forms lines of varying shaped bosses separated by plain ridges. The cape was probably lined with leather and stiffened internally at the base with a strip of sheet bronze, fragments of which survive. The ceremonial nature of the cape is confirmed by the fact that when in position it is impossible to use the upper arms. Height 9.3 in (23.5 cm)

Pottery for the living, urns for the dead

Occasionally in the Wessex graves as we have seen a small decorated cup was added, more rarely a larger vessel. Over much of the rest of Britain the custom of placing some form of pot in the grave became firmly established, and this is often the only object found with the dead. Native potters under the stimulus of the new Beaker technology had responded by producing a new range of flat-based forms. Amongst these was a group of related small bowls and vases collectively known as Food 45 Vessels. Some of the smaller versions rival in the care lavished on their decoration the best of Beaker pottery, and some of the motifs and the use of a toothed-comb stamp to create them mirror Beaker usages. Yet the thick walls and poor firing of many underline a less developed technological skill and knowledge. Food Vessels are found with both inhumed remains and with cremations. Other groups preferred cremation and this mode of burial was to become the dominant rite of the period throughout the British Isles. Many forms of storage vessel were pressed into service to act as containers for the cremated bones or to 46

accompany them, the most widespread being the Collared Vessel, found over much of the United Kingdom as well as northern and eastern Ireland. This too displays a clear development out of the old Peterborough tradition. Unlike the pottery which had gone before and most of the contemporary Food Vessel styles, Collared Vessels carry only restrained decoration confined in the main to the upper half of the vessel and frequently to the collar and rim alone. Restrained decoration is equally characteristic of the contemporary Cordoned Urns of northern Britain and Ireland. The Cordoned Urn is in essence a simple broad-based bucket-shaped vessel whose outer surface has been broken into zones by the addition of applied strips of clay. Only the Food Vessel Urn, often identical in form and decoration to its namesake but of larger size, retains the earlier taste for heavy ornamentation. In Ireland especially, exuberant decorative schemes were favoured incorporating incised and corded ornament enhanced by complex motifs made with applied strips of clay, suggesting a survival or re-

46 A range of vessels used as urns: (from left to right) Trevisker-style Urn from Tregeseal, St Just-in-Penwith, Cornwall; Enlarged Food Vessel Urn from Prudhoe, Northumberland; Cordoned Urn from Colwinston, Glamorgan and Collared Urn from Lake, Wiltshire. Largest vessel 21 in (53.5 cm) high.

45 A range of Food Vessels (left to right) a Yorkshire Vase from Goodmanham, Humberside; a Ridged Vase from Sturminster Marshall, Dorset; an Irish bowl (inverted to show decoration on the base) from Ireland; an Irish Vase from Co. Antrim and a Tripartite Vase from Kilmartin, Argyll, maximum diameter of Bowl 6 in (15.3 cm)

47 A range of Deverel-Rimbury pottery from southern and eastern England: (from left to right) Globular Urn from Littleton Down, Dorset with incised decoration; Barrel Urn from Pokesdown, Bournemouth, Dorset with vertical plain cordons; Globular Urn from Milborne St Andrew, Dorset, with horizontal finger-tip rilling; Bucket Urn with heavy finger-tip impressed decoration in the 'Ardleigh' style from Brantham, Suffolk and Bucket Urn with finger-tipped cordon and rim from Broxbourne, Hertfordshire. Height of Ardleigh type Urn 16.9 in (43 cm)

emergence of Grooved Ware tastes. In the south, vigorous cross-channel movement between south-eastern England, northern France and the Low Countries had led to the appearance on both sides of the Channel of biconical vessels sometimes decorated with applied 'horse-shoe' handles. Partly in response to these influences a new range of pottery was developed in southern and eastern England.

Vessels of this Deverel-Rimbury tradition 47 show considerable local variation and forms range from fine narrow-mouthed globular vases often decorated with incised patterns or with finger-tip rilling to thick-walled, coarse, bucket-shaped vessels decorated, if at all, with a single horizontal finger-tipped cordon or a row of finger-tip impressions on the rim. Exceptionally, as in the Ardleigh group in East Anglia, finger-tip decoration can cover the entire surface or be used to form simple patterns. The large thin barrel-shaped vessels are of particular interest for these sometimes carry applied vertical cordons showing again

48 Detail of impressed decoration made with a plaited cord. This was in relatively rare and only sporadic use for pottery decoration except in south-west England where it was particularly favoured during the period 1800–1500 bc.

49 A range of Accessory Cups: (from the left) a perforated wall cup from Bulford, Wiltshire; miniature food vessel from Ireland, vertical walled cup from N. Newbald, Humberside; miniature Collared Urn from Northamptonshire and converging mouth cup from Clifton, Greater Manchester. Diam. of perforated cup 3.2 in (8.1 cm)

50 *above*. Detail of decoration on the jet necklace from Melfort, Argyll. The pin-pricks create a pattern which can be read either as a running plain chevron or as groups of opposed triangles. This type of ambiguous pattern is common on Beaker pottery. Compare pl. *27 far right*. The largest of the spacer-plates is 2 in (5 cm)

52 Bronze dagger of earlier Wessex type and decorated bone pin found with a skeleton at Brough, Humberside. The bone pin is an insular adaptation of a multiple-ring-headed form then in fashion in Central Europe. Length of dagger 6.7 in (17 cm). Length of pin 2.4 in (6 cm)

survival of Grooved Ware decorative tastes. Already south-western England is marked out as a separate province producing its own distinctive range of wares. The earlier vessels, sometimes provided with a pair or even four strap handles to span the shoulder, often carry plaited cord decoration on their upper half. 48 Later forms continue the range of patterns but cord is abandoned in favour of incising the designs into the surface of the clay. Sometimes associated with the urns but more frequently, as in Wessex, the only pottery to be placed in the grave is a series of small Accessory Cups. 49 These range over a wide spectrum from the very simple and plain to the elaborate and decorated. Some are simply miniature versions of Food Vessels and Urns, others perhaps reflect cup forms in daily domestic use.

Custom appears to have dictated that little other than pottery was interred with the majority of the dead. A few graves in northern Britain contain multi-strand necklaces of jet, 50 the counterpart of those in Wessex made of amber. Beads, buttons, pendants and sometimes ear plugs, rarely of faience or amber, more often of jet or bone are occasionally 51 found, along with bone copies of imported metal pins. Modest items of personal use – flint 52 knives, arrowheads or scrapers, a small bronze knife, awl or razor – with but few exceptions – complete the list. Only a handful of graves with stone battleaxe or much more rarely, a bronze dagger, suggest comparison with the wealth of the later Wessex graves. Less still was placed with the Deverel-Rimbury dead in the south, where the presence of even a single metallic object is a rare event.

Two factors suggest, however, that we should be wary of taking such evidence at face value, for how many objects in the grave, made of wood or cloth, basketry or leather have perished? Only rarely do conditions allow such evidence to survive but that evidence gradually mounts. In 1834 a barrow at Gris-

51 Bone beads found in a grave at Folkton, N. Yorkshire also containing a food vessel, flint scraper and bronze awl. The patterns on the beads have been made by charring. Length of bead 0.6 in (1.5 cm)

thorpe in Yorkshire revealed a waterlogged oak coffin with a lid, one end of which had been carved. The coffin contained, along with the body, an assortment of objects including a bronze knife with bone pommel and flints. Of greater interest were a small dish made of strips of bark sewn together with animal sinew, a wooden pin, a double conjoined ring of horn and the remains of the animal skin in which the body had been wrapped, secured at the breast by a bone pin. Another barrow, Loose Howe, set high on the Yorkshire Moors above the head of Rosedale, was examined in 1937. Beneath this lay the waterlogged remains of boat-shaped trough, coffin and lid made of oak. The coffin had contained a body. Traces of cloth still clung to one ankle and a fragment of sewn leather shoe was also recovered. That the burial had been made during the autumn was shown by the presence of hazel husks and branches, and enough survived to show that the body had been placed upon a bed of rushes, reeds or straw. Such instances do not provide the wealth of information offered by similar but better preserved graves in Denmark but they serve as another timely reminder that what survives elsewhere is mainly the inorganic residue winnowed by decay. In reality the populace would by now have worn garments of woven cloth with warmer cloaks made from animal skins, and with wrappings or leather sandals on their feet. The basket and the skin bag must surely have been in widespread use, particularly for travel, as would containers made from bark or wood. The Wilsford Shaft provides a further narrow window into this world. Here a vertical shaft nearly two metres across had been sunk to a depth of over thirty metres through the solid chalk. From the lower filling of this were recovered broken Deverel-Rimbury pottery and rope and with them fragments of stave-built tubs, of wooden bowl and of stitched containers also made of wood.

Over much of Britain the burial rites and monuments with which many of these finds are associated show a bewildering variation, and in detail often differ over quite short distances. In the north and west round barrows, ring and platform cairns, flat cemeteries and simple unmarked graves are but a few of the ways now chosen to honour the dead. Within the overall belief that inhumation, or later and more universally cremation, was appropriate, local preferences are everywhere apparent. In the south the picture is somewhat different for here there is a more marked tendency for burials to be made in groups set into existing barrows or for clusters of flat graves to be grouped together to form large flat cemeteries sometimes numbering more than a hundred interments. Indeed it seems likely that in these clusters, which include burials of both sexes and all ages, we can see the burial grounds of small individual families.

The uptake of new land

Our knowledge of settlements and farms during the second half of the second millennium, though still patchy, is now increasing rapidly. On the chalklands of southern England the average farming family lived in a circular timber-framed house entered through a short rectangular porch. Ancillary huts provided space for a variety of household and farming activities including weaving, storage and the preparation of food. Usually the characteristic sub-rectangular embanked or bank-and-ditch enclosure embraces more than one of these living units implying that the farm was being worked, not by a single but by an extended family. Where the evidence still survives tracks and droveways can be seen linking the enclosure to nearby fields and pasturage. The farm régime was based on cereal cultivation (wheat and barley) as well as stock rearing (cattle and sheep) the animals being provided with lean-to shelters against the huts.

On the uplands the picture is somewhat different, for though there is widespread evidence for cereal cultivation, greater emphasis was placed on stock. In the south-west, on Dartmoor and on Bodmin Moor, circular stone-built houses are the rule. These often replace earlier timber-framed structures as though lowland farmers were adapting to the harsher realities of upland conditions. Where agriculture was more important the houses nestle amidst the rectilinear stone-walled fields, but in areas geared more to stock-raising the houses are often grouped together enclosed within a stone-walled 'pound', a few reaching the size of a small village.

Only recently have we begun to appreciate on just what a scale land allotments were conceived. On Dartmoor the stone 'reaves' which mark out the main land divisions can run for miles sometimes ignoring natural features like steep-sided valleys, and all appear to be of similar date. We must therefore conclude that much of Dartmoor was enclosed over a relatively short period of time as a single agreed act. Similar extensive systems have been recovered elsewhere, on the Fen edge for example at Fengate outside Peterborough and on the river gravels. In other parts of upland Britain evidence accumulates for further settlements of Dartmoor type. Comparable hut circles and enclosures are now known from north-east England in the Cheviots and Teesdale, southern Scotland and areas of Wales, sometimes set within enclosures, elsewhere arranged in lines following the contour of the hill-slope. Another frequent feature of the landscape dating to this period are groups of small cairns marking the initial clearance of stone from the adjoining land. Yet, despite the evidence of Dartmoor and for extensive division of lands over much of southern Britain little survives in the archaeological record outside Wessex to suggest a hierarchical society. Settlements show few signs of distinction between one dwelling and the next and rich burials are notably absent. The impression given is one of growing prosperity and a rising population; of the uptake of new land and of increasingly flourishing bronze-workers stimulated at least in the south-east by contact maintained with their counterparts in north-west France, supplying the needs of an increasingly affluent society.

The palstave had become the predominant 53 axe form in the south made at first with a broad flaring blade, later to be narrowed and given a side loop to assist in hafting. The north preferred the haft-flanged axe. These two types took the axe form mounted in a split elbow-haft very much to the end of its logical refinement. As implements both would have been highly efficient for woodworking and for breaking new ground but both required large quantities of metal. Later developments were to concentrate on reducing this requirement. In weaponry the bronze dagger was replaced by the dirk and rapier. At the same time the 54

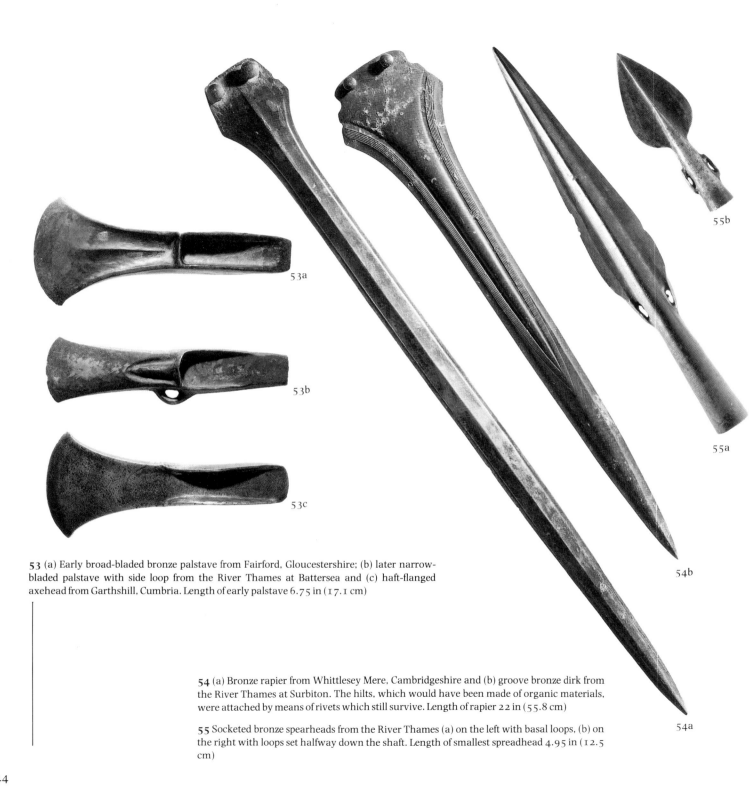

53 (a) Early broad-bladed bronze palstave from Fairford, Gloucestershire; (b) later narrow-bladed palstave with side loop from the River Thames at Battersea and (c) haft-flanged axehead from Garthshill, Cumbria. Length of early palstave 6.75 in (17.1 cm)

54 (a) Bronze rapier from Whittlesey Mere, Cambridgeshire and (b) groove bronze dirk from the River Thames at Surbiton. The hilts, which would have been made of organic materials, were attached by means of rivets which still survive. Length of rapier 22 in (55.8 cm)

55 Socketed bronze spearheads from the River Thames (a) on the left with basal loops, (b) on the right with loops set halfway down the shaft. Length of smallest spreadhead 4.95 in (12.5 cm)

56 A range of bronze ornaments, many showing Continental inspiration (from left to right) quoit-headed pin from East Dean, Sussex; ribbed-pin from the River Thames at Kingston; decorated pin with perforation through the widest part of the shank from the River Thames at Wandsworth; a twisted neck-ring and spiral finger ring from a hoard found at Hollingbury Hill, Sussex and a bracelet of a type known as a 'Sussex loop' from Handcross, Sussex. Length of longest pin 11.4 in (28.8 cm)

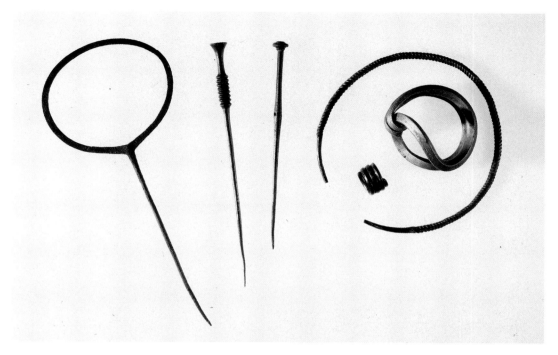

57 Gold twisted bar torc from Stanton, Staffordshire. Torcs of this type vary considerably in size and may not all have served the same purpose, some being worn round the neck, others being large enough to have been worn round the waist. Those found coiled, like the one from Stanton, could be arm ornaments, though the coiling might have been done simply to make the torc more compact for concealment. Length as coiled 4.25 in (11.3 cm)

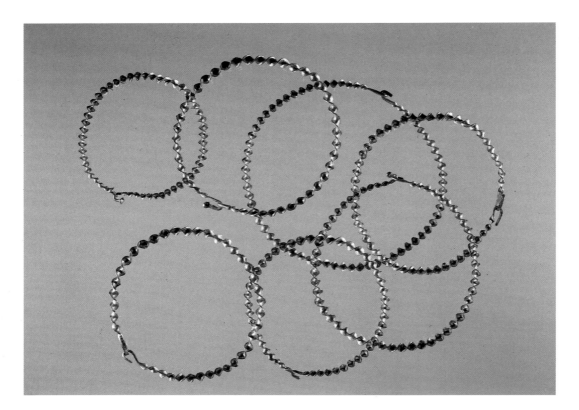

58 A group of gold twisted ribbon bracelets, part of a hoard of some forty, found in 1857 on Law Farm, Urquhart, Morayshire. This type of ornament occurs mainly in Scotland and Ireland. Diam. of largest bracelet 5.2 in (15.2 cm)

hafting of the socketed spearhead was improv- 55 ed by the addition of side loops to the socket to allow thongs to be passed through, the design being later improved further by placing these at the base of the socket. The metal smiths of north Wales played an important part in these developments, using for a while a new alloy, leaded bronze, whose full potential was to be appreciated and exploited only at a later stage.

Inspired by trends on the Continent a new range of personal ornament was produced for the southern British market, some copying Continental types, others developed to suit local tastes. Twisted bronze neckrings, brace- 56 lets, spiral and plain finger rings and new forms of ornamental pin all now make their appearance. Significant new items were also added to the range of tool produced. The knobbed sickle was introduced along with the first metal saw and socketed hammer. Though manufactured locally, much of the bronze came from abroad, not directly but in the form of recycled metal derived from melting down earlier imports. This re-use of metal was a crucial factor in extending the availability of bronze to an increasingly wider section of the community. In Ireland, goldsmiths in parti-cular were now beginning to produce some of their finest work, culminating in the develop-ment of the twisted bar torc, a masterpiece of 57 their craft, while in Scotland a more slender form of twisted ribbon bracelet was much in 58 favour. Relatively few of these metal objects reached the grave or remain to be found in the excavated settlements for when these were abandoned most of the ornaments, tools and weapons were gathered up, too valuable to be left behind.

60 Early form of bronze leaf-shaped slashing sword from the River Thames at Brentford. Length 24.5 in (62 cm)

Changes spiritual and temporal

An increasing population and progressive exhaustion of large areas of arable land, however, finally took its toll. Much marginal land could no longer be worked. Crop failure and starvation must have been ever present threats for by 1000 bc the climate too was becoming significantly colder and wetter, necessitating in Somerset the construction of new trackways in the low lying levels. The higher lands previously under cultivation suffered most. With worsening conditions blanket peat began to grow and farming of areas like Dartmoor and the North Yorkshire Moors had to be abandoned. In many areas a new authoritarian control becomes apparent, while weaponry, both functional and for display becomes ever more prominent in the archaeological record. It was no doubt pressure on land and the need to safeguard food supplies that forced these social changes. In lowland Britain there is now a shift towards larger settlement and the rich chalk lands of Wessex see new land divisions created by long linear dykes cutting across the earlier field systems. To this phase belong many of the earliest hilltop settlements and defended enclosures designed to provide both refuge and safe storage for communal food supplies. Elsewhere new types of settlement were established like that at Runnymede set on an island on the River Thames strategically placed to control a major route for trade. Here and there large timber-framed round houses appear, twelve or more metres across, set within their own circular enclosures, marking the dwellings of an élite. A pronounced shift in the basis of religion is also to be seen. If much of third millennium belief had hung upon the power of the dead, of fertility and the mysteries of regeneration, much of the second had been concerned with observation of the sun and moon. A worsening climate with increasing cloud cover now removed the mechanism by which such beliefs could be perpetuated.

Wetter weather and swelling lakes and rivers were now to usher in the religious beliefs which came to dominate the millennium before Christ and these were about water and what dwelt therein. Many of the old ways of honouring the dead fall out of use. In the south the great flat cemeteries cease to be constructed. In the north barrow-building was to survive fitfully here and there for some centuries, but in most areas the custom of formal burial in a marked grave ceases to be followed.

By this time too Britain was feeling the outer ripples of events which had first begun in Central Europe. The influence of the *Urnfield* Warriors had spread rapidly and, at first or second hand, many of their trappings – slashing swords, curved knives, metal arrowheads and shields – began to reach these shores. The new swords in particular created great interest and the native bronzesmiths now began a series of experiments to copy the new form culminating in the first native slashing swords with leaf-shaped blades. Yet the Urnfield pressure as represented by metalwork and new forms of fine, thin-walled, sometimes decorated pottery was not felt everywhere. Its presence is largely confined to south-eastern England, particularly the Valley of the Thames, to southern Wales and Ireland. If raiding parties or actual settlers reached these shores then their number is unlikely to have been great, for it was not long before the strong ties between south-eastern England and north-west France, which had remained at the fringe of the Urnfield world, began to re-assert themselves. The recent discovery of a cargo of bronze implements and scrap mainly of French type lying at the bottom of the sea just outside the modern harbour at Dover, in Langdon Bay, offers vivid testimony to that contact. Though nothing remained of the vessel itself, finds of actual boats from North Ferriby and Brigg in Humberside dating either side of the Dover wreck show that stout plank-

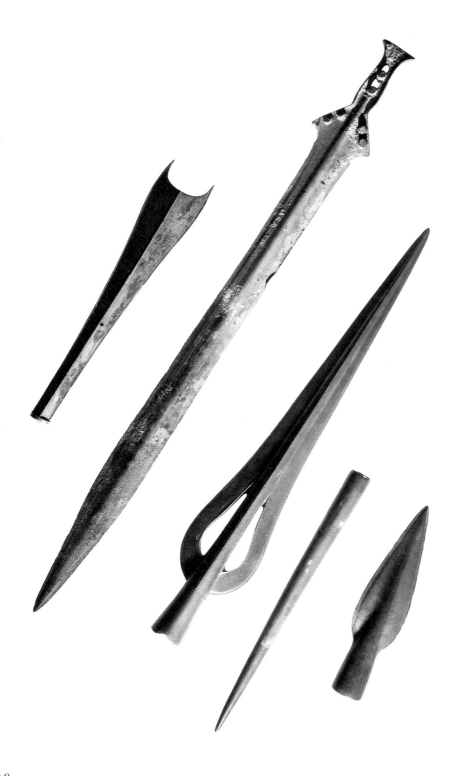

built ships up to fifteen metres long were already in use, while the nature of the bronzes recovered shows clearly that on this occasion the cargo carried was inward bound.

Given these contacts, it is not surprising that the next major technological development should occur simultaneously on both sides of the Channel – the adoption of a new alloy to form lead-bronze. The great advantage of adding lead, up to 7% of the mix, was that it reduced the melting point and allowed the metal when molten to flow more freely into the mould. This in turn opened the way to casting a new range of thin-walled items such as the hollow-bladed spearhead and the sword chape. At least in the south and east bronze now became available in some quantity, though these new developments were slow to reach the rest of Britain where the bronze-smiths continued for some time to fashion implements in the old tin-bronze. In the Fenland and the Thames Valley finds of swords and spears now become much more common and with them comes evidence for the more extensive recycling of bronze. This takes the form of heaps of scrap metal often already broken down into pieces of a size suitable for re-melting. Being heavy and valuable, these scrap metal hoards were hidden in the ground

59 Bronze shield found in a bog at Moel Siabod, near Capel Curig, Caernarvonshire. Decoration consists of concentric rows of small bosses alternating with raised ribs, beaten out from the back. The type is British and shows considerable elaboration away from Continental forms. Diam. 25.35 in (64.4 cm)

61 Range of bronze weapons, all from the River Thames (from the top) tongue-shaped chape for protecting the end of a sword scabbard, at Kingston; leaf-shaped sword of developed form, at Wandsworth; socketed spearhead with lunate openings in the blade, at Battersea; socketed ferrule for the end of a spear-shaft, at Isleworth and a leaf shaped socketed spearhead, at Taplow. Length of sword 23.2 in (58.8 cm)

49

62 *top.* Different forms of Bronze socketed axe, (top) South Welsh from Cats Hole Cave, Ilston, Glamorgan. Irish bag shaped from Clone, Co Kilkenny, (bottom). Yorkshire type from Lowthorpe, Humberside and faceted from Newham, Northumberland. Length of faceted axe 4.65 in (11.8 cm)

63 *far right.* Bronze side-blow horn from Dunmanway, Co. Cork. The origin of this type lies in musical instruments made from the actual horns of an animal. The horn would originally have had a wooden or bone mouth piece set into the mouth hole and was capable of producing only a single note. Length 24 in (61 cm)

64 *above.* A selection of bronze crotals or rattle-bells from the Dowris hoard, Co. Offaly. Largest, excluding terminal ring is 5 in (12.8 cm)

usually well away from obvious settlement and presumably marked, for many acted as metal banks to be added to or withdrawn from as the bronze was required. The largest of these hoards, found by chance in the Cambridgeshire Fens at Isleham, consisted of over 6500 separate pieces of bronze placed within an old storage vessel set in the ground.

It is from these collections of scrap metal in particular that we can gain a better impression of the full range of metal objects now being made and from this a glimpse of the society which had use of them. We are left in no doubt that the age of the warrior had already dawned. There is more than a hint too of an emerging social structure in which the sword-bearer stood above the spearman and both above the peasant. Swords and tongue-shaped scabbard chapes; spearheads in profusion, many of simple leaf shape but others 61 more elaborate with lunate openings in their blades; long tubular ferrules to protect and balance the spear shaft, are all in plentiful supply. Cauldrons made from sheets of bronze riveted together and flesh hooks to claw the meat from the boiling broth were fashioned for the feast, while horsebits and harness fittings along with parts for wheeled vehicles show the horse to be firmly in the service of at least the higher echelons of society.

By 700 bc this new leaded-bronze technology had spread throughout the British Isles bringing to all parts a greater abundance both of metal and range of implement. Here at last was the age of bronze, for now a profusion of regional forms of socketed axe appear together 62 with socketed knives and sickles; gouges, saws and chisels for the woodworker; hammers and punches for the metal smiths and for the warrior, new forms of spear and sword. In Ireland superb side-blow horns were being 63 manufactured as well as crotals, no doubt to 64 bedeck the necks of prize cattle in parade. The finest cauldrons and buckets also date from 65

65 Bronze cauldron from the River Thames near Battersea. The cauldron is made of sheets of bronze held together with dome-headed rivets, and has two swing handles. Cauldrons and buckets surviving from this period often show heavy patching and clearly enjoyed a long period of use. Diam. 22.5 in (57 cm)

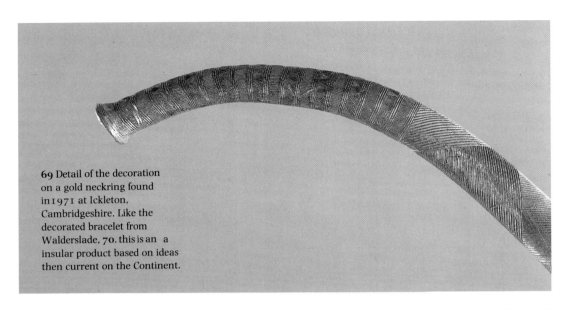

69 Detail of the decoration on a gold neckring found in 1971 at Ickleton, Cambridgeshire. Like the decorated bracelet from Walderslade, **70**. this is an an insular product based on ideas then current on the Continent.

66 *bottom left*. Typical components of a scrap metal hoard including a carp's tongue sword (usually found broken into short lengths); to the right, whole and fragmentary winged axes; on the left a hog-backed knife, bugle-shaped harness fittings and pieces of copper ingot. Length of sword 23.5 in (59.6 cm)

67 *below*. Ceremonial bronze spearhead from the Plaistow Marshes, London. The blade which is hollow would have been attached to a wooden shaft by means of the transverse peg found below the barbs. This peg, perhaps for the attachment of ribbons or other decoration, which protrudes each side of the socket, renders the barbs useless. Length 10.75 in (27.2 cm)

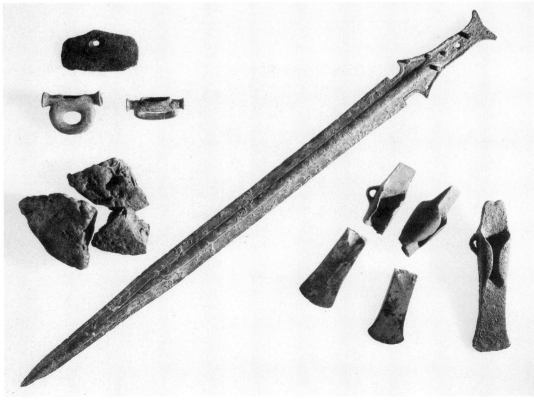

this phase. To sustain this expanding market new sources of metal needed to be sought. Scrap was imported in bulk from north-west France so that the metal hoards of south-eastern England now become full of fragments of Continental types – Carp's tongue swords, a parallel-sided form narrowing to an elongated tip as though intended as much for thrusting as for slashing; winged axes, hog-backed knives and an array of harness and baldrick fittings.

While much of this material was destined to be recycled to produce new weapons and tools, a proportion was taken out of circulation by ritual deposition either of objects deliberately fashioned for such a purpose or of functional weaponry so assigned. Thus in the Thames Valley and following an arc down from the Humber through the Welsh Marches to Devon, hoards of non-functional, broad, hollow-bladed barbed spearheads were placed in rivers, marshes and other watery places, while particularly in northern England and much of Scotland functional swords were similarly offered.

The goldsmiths too were hard at work in Ireland producing a vast array of bracelets, dress fasteners, tress rings, cuff fasteners and, most splendid of all, sumptuous gorgets to be worn around the neck. Some of these were to find their way to Britain while the British smiths in turn developed other forms of neck

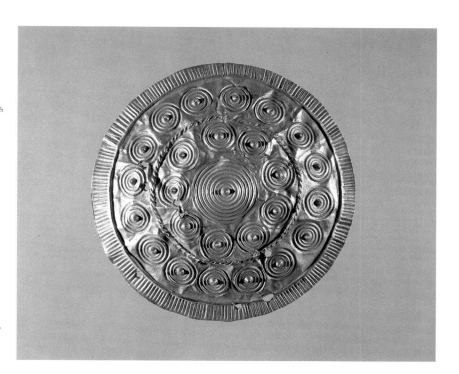

68 Terminal disc of a gold gorget from Ireland, showing detailed repoussé decoration. Diam. 2.75 in (7 cm)

70 Two gold bracelets found together in 1965 at Walderslade, Kent. The undecorated bracelet with trumpet terminals is an Irish type. The second bracelet with everted terminals and concentric circle decoration is an insular adaptation of a bronze bracelet of Continental Urnfield type. Diam. of decorated bracelet 2.9 in (7.3 cm)

ring and bracelet to satisfy more local tastes.
Of the life of the smith himself little can be pieced together though the Heathery Burn cave near Stanhope in Co. Durham offers a rare glimpse of this world. Here spread along the length of a passage running deep into the rock lay traces of his life and work – weapons, some already broken down ready for re-melting, a fragment of metal ingot, half of a bronze mould for casting socketed axes.

knives, a pair of tongs, bracelets of bronze, jet and gold, simple plain pottery, a bronze bucket and wood-working tools as well as axle mounts for a wheeled vehicle, harness fittings and antler cheek pieces – not so different in range to the things that lie around the tempor-ary camp of a tinker of more modern times.

70

71

71 A selection of objects from the Heathery Burn Cave, Co. Durham: Harness fittings in the form of bronze discs and rings, cheek-pieces for horsebits made of antler and (on the right) four bronze nave bands for a wheeled vehicle. Largest disc 5.7 in (14.5 cm) across.

The arrival of iron

By 700 BC (600 bc) – for now we can begin to move from carbon dates to calendar years – the rise of the *Hallstatt* warrior lords had set in motion new and far-reaching events. Under their patronage, iron-working was to spread rapidly across Europe. By the middle of this century long swords of Hallstatt type accom- 72 panied by scabbards ornamented with winged chapes, appear in the Thames Valley, in eastern Scotland and in Ireland. These were of bronze and many are of local make for they differ somewhat from the Continental pattern, but fast on their heels came the blacksmiths. For Britain the age of iron had at last arrived.

Given the new technology that iron-working required it is difficult to believe that its introduction would have been quite so swift and total had not Hallstatt lords themselves provided a compelling impetus for its adoption. For the native bronze industries its coming was dramatic and quickly terminal. In south-east England in particular vast deposits of scrap metal dating from this time took a major part of the bronze supply out of circulation. It was never again required, for the mass market which had developed for bronze implements and weapons quickly collapsed. For a while the bronzesmiths still found customers for a basic range of tool and new forms of large socketed axe were developed decorated with rib and pellet ornament. In an attempt to keep alive the market in swords of native type, 'Hallstatt' features were even 73 added, but the swift adoption of iron could not be halted. With its coming the long-distance trading networks which had been set up to ensure that a steady supply of metal reached the bronzesmiths fell into disuse and for a period Britain enjoyed a spell of relative isolation.

Far more is known about farming and settlement during the last six centuries or so of the first millennium BC than for any period that had gone before. The mass of evidence

72 Bronze Hallstatt 'C' sword from the River Tyne below Newcastle and winged scabbard chape from the River Thames at Wandsworth. Length of sword 27.25 in (69.2 cm)

from simple hut to large well-ordered village is immense: shape and plan differing in form from region to region reflecting local taste as much as local need, for isolation brought with it fragmentation. Thousands of acres of fields have been mapped with attendant droveways and dykes leaving no doubt that in areas where this could be pursued farming was now intensive. At its base lay a regime founded on cattle, sheep and cereals though local conditions would often have dictated what emphasis was placed upon the individual components of that mix. Hulled barley and spelt became prominent as cereal crops, no doubt because both could be winter sown, but club wheat and more rarely rye were also grown. The benefits of manuring were by now well understood and the need to return to the soil some of the fertility which repeated cropping constantly drained. Yet for much of the higher lands of the north and west that realisation had come too late and many an attractive landscape of the present in the Pennines, Lake District or Scottish Uplands is largely the product of the over-cultivation and over-grazing that took place in prehistoric times.

At first the period saw much unrest. In many areas farm, settlement and village was now set within a defensive palisade or earth- 74 work. Hillforts, still a prominent feature of the modern landscape, were constructed in some numbers. Well over a thousand are known, some modest, others enclosing more than one hundred acres; some of simple bank-and-ditch construction, others seeking defence in depth against the sling with line upon line of massive rampart. Many of these cluster densely in the West Midlands from the Cotswolds to the Welsh Marches and many too dominate the chalk downs of central southern England. More were built in North Wales and in nothern England. Yet hillforts are not to be found everywhere. Over much of eastern England there are few and in other regions other forms

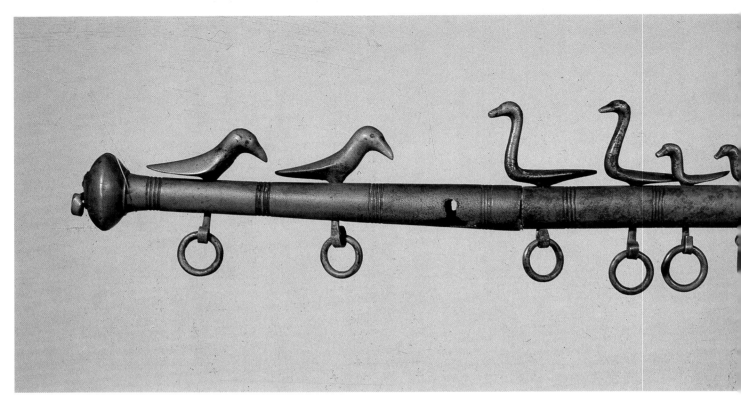

of site prevail: in the south west the cliff castle and the round; in Northumberland and southern Scotland the palisaded enclosure, in north-west Scotland the stone-built *Dun*, *Broch* and *Wheelhouse*. It would be wrong to assume that all such sites met the same needs or that these did not change over time, but it is difficult not to feel that while in some areas the pressure to fortify to meet actual attack or simply to impress formed an essential element of life, other regions enjoyed a much freer, less dramatic existence in which major fortress had no place. In some well-studied areas we can begin to see in the restricted circulation of certain types of article the emergence of tribal territories which were to persist into historic times; in others the situation remained fluid as power and influence waxed and waned. Certainly in southern England many of the

75

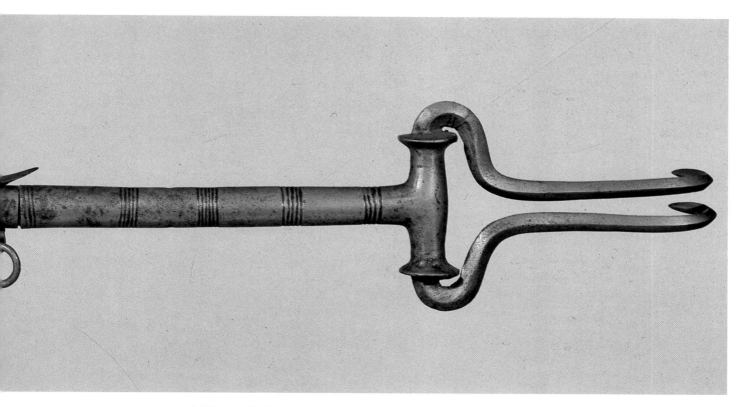

73 *above*. Bronze flesh hook from Dunaverney, Co. Antrim. The handle, hollow and in three parts, would have fitted round a wooden shaft. A family of water birds and a pair of ravens have been added in decoration and the pendant rings would once have held metal jangles. Both the jangles and the water birds suggest that this piece belongs to the period when strong Hallstatt influences were being felt. Length as illustrated 22.4 in (56.3 cm)

74 *left*. Aerial photograph of the hillfort of Maiden Castle, Dorset showing multiple ramparts and complex entrances.

hillforts which had been built in Wessex had but a short existence, for by 400 BC most had been abandoned leaving only a few, like Danebury, to show expansion and to become centres for administration and the regulation of commerce, dominating the territory around. Those that remained often show remodelled defences replacing earlier ditch and stone- or timber-faced ramparts with a form presenting an unbroken slope from ditch bottom to top of bank, with gauntlet entrance or ones of deep meandering complexity.

But though hillforts and stone-built structures are the most obvious and impressive monuments to survive from this period, aerial photography has revealed that much of the population lived elsewhere. Amidst the arable fields and pastures are many smaller sites of enclosed and unenclosed farmsteads 76

and crofts. At Walesland Rath near Haverford West in Pembrokeshire one such farm has been excavated with its main circular buildings many times rebuilt at the centre of a penannular bank-and-ditch enclosure with associated farm buildings set along the inside of the bank. In contrast other sites like Gussage-All-Saints in Dorset have shown on excavation major changes in use and layout over time. Much would have depended upon local needs. In many parts the timber-framed round house, often with short entrance porch, remained the principal form of dwelling, but rectangular long houses were built within the fort at Crickley Hill in rows suggesting here a more ordered village life. Characteristic of many of these sites are pits and settings of four, six or eight posts. Pits were used extensively for the storage of grain for if the pit was tightly

75 The Broch of Mousa, Shetlands. The Broch still stands to a height of 43 ft (13 m). Within the thickness of the walls are concealed small chambers and a staircase giving access to higher levels.

76 A range of hand-made vessels in use from the fourth to the second centuries bc, found at Little Woodbury, Wiltshire and Park Brow, Sussex. Height of central vessel 10 in (25.4 cm)

77 Four of the iron objects found in the River Lea at Waltham Abbey, Essex (from left to right) a pair of tongs, a socketed hammer, a rasp and an anvil equipped with grooves to act also as a swage. Length of rasp 9.15 in (23.2 cm)

sealed the natural build-up of carbon dioxide within prevented decay and destroyed small predators. Such storage was admirably suited to the keeping of seed corn where there was no need to break the seal for many months. Cereals for everyday consumption would have been kept elsewhere: small amounts in pottery or wooden storage vessels or in leather bags, with the main store above ground in store-houses whose only trace would be the settings of post-holes which alone survive. Fodder too must similarly have been kept. As to how the cereal was processed for eating, there is little actual evidence. The rotary handmill was now available to replace the former saddle quern for grinding the corn into flour but there is little trace of the clay ovens needed to turn this into bread. Yet in the waterlogged deposits at Glastonbury actual bread does survive, coarse by modern standards, made from wheat, barley and wild oats still mixed with traces of the weeds which had grown within the host crop. The crop itself was now harvested with the aid

of sickles made of iron, and iron too was beginning to be used to cap the wooden share of the *ard* and perhaps too for its coulter.

The speed with which iron had joined wood as the principal material for tools and implements in everyday use owed more to the ubiquity of the iron ores than to the ease with which these could be converted into metal. The ore had first to be broken and smelted with charcoal in a furnace, the resulting bloom then forged into whatever shape was required by repeated hammering when red hot. If we could observe him the blacksmith of the period would differ little from his counterpart in historic times. Many of the tools needed – the long-handled tongs to hold the red hot metal, the hammers and anvils for shaping, the rasps for trimming and pokers for riddling the fire can all be found fashioned by the blacksmith for his own use, like those from the River Lea 77 at Waltham Abbey, Essex. Tools for other use included saws, gouges, knives and shears and the warrior was provided with spear and sword. The long swords in particular are masterpieces of their craft, and perhaps the product of specialist sword smiths, for some carry a maker's stamp upon their blades. But while iron became the principal metal for weapons and objects of utility, the finest items for decoration and display were still to be fashioned in bronze, more rarely gold, and many were enhanced with an art style which though introduced from the Continent was to see its finest achievements in the work of craftsmen working in Britain in the century or so before the Roman Invasion of AD43.

Early Celtic art at its inception had owed much to Greek art incorporating many of its more familiar elements like palmettes and lotus flowers, but the power of Celtic art lay in the ability to develop these motifs into ever more abstract flowing forms. To achieve the required effect, the artist called upon a range of techniques either engraving or chasing the

patterns into the surface of the metal or modelling the designs three-dimensionally in wax for casting into metal via the lost-wax process. Three-dimensional patterns could also be worked up in repoussé giving the art style a remarkable flexibility and subtlety of form which, in its finest expression, rivals anything achieved elsewhere or since in the realms of abstract art.

Much effort was given over to the decoration of objects of parade, the scabbard and the shield receiving considerable attention. Most scabbards and shields would have been of wood or leather but the finest were faced with bronze. Some like the scabbards from the bog at Lisnacrogher, Co. Antrim or the splendid 78 facing plate for another found at Bugthorpe, 79 Yorkshire were decorated over their entire length with delicate scroll and tendril patterns. Shields were oval, the hand-grip spanning a central hole covered by a protective boss. Only in Britain do complete bronze facings for such shields survive. The spectacular Batter- 80 sea Shield is made from four bronze sheets attached originally to a shield of wood by means of binding strips along the edge. The central boss is framed by a circular roundel with similar but smaller roundels set above and below, all made in repoussé. Smaller roundels form a prominent feature of the flowing palmette and scroll design and these are further enhanced by inlays of red glass. The somewhat earlier Witham Shield is of two 81 bronze sheets with overlying ornament comprising decorated central boss and upper and lower roundels joined together by a narrow spine, all cast in one piece. Whether contemporary with this design or marking an earlier use, the outline of a boar can still be detected on the metal sheets. Presumably this had been of bronze for the rivet holes by which it was attached are clearly visible. Britain too 82 can claim the only horned helmet of bronze to survive from the Celtic world, found near

80 The Battersea Shield. Found in the River Thames at Battersea in 1857. Length 30.6 in (77.7 cm)

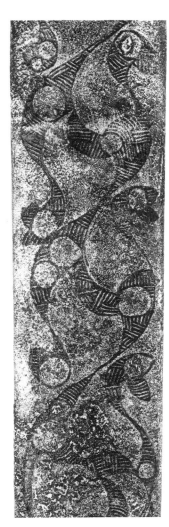

Waterloo Bridge in the very heart of London. Many of these pieces, which must surely have been prized items in their day, come from rivers or from areas once lake or marsh, and though some were perhaps lost in battle or in river crossing, the majority call for different explanation: as offerings made to placate or thank the water deities.

Only rarely has fine metalwork been found in such a context as to shed light upon the society which owned and had use of it. Little has come from hillfort or settlement and until the first century BC little reached the grave, for until that time only in eastern Yorkshire was much in the way of formal burial practised and then by a community which was at least in part immigrant from the Continent.

In eastern Yorkshire the dead were interred in cemeteries often of vast size, the majority placed crouched beneath a small square-ditched barrow accompanied, if at all, by a single pot, a joint of pork, a simple brooch of bronze, more often iron, shaped like a modern kilt-pin, or other minor trinket. In some cemeteries, like that at Burton Fleming, we can also see the graves of warriors, layed out at full length with their iron swords, but all contrast with a mere handful of richer burials, mostly interred with the remains of two-wheeled carts found amidst and on the fringes of this region. Whether these differed in any material way from the war-chariots which Caesar was to note later in his account of his expeditionary force to south-eastern England it is impossible to say but the Yorkshire burials offer the best insight available into the type of vehicle Caesar might have seen. Each was equipped with a pair of twelve-spoked wheels, shod with an outer tyre of iron, the wheels secured to the axle by means of linch pins usually of iron sometimes ornamented with bronze. To the axle too was attached a central pole implying that the cart was drawn by a pair of horses and such a pair were found beneath the 'King's

78 *left* Decorated bronze scabbard plate from Lisnacrogher, Co. Antrim. Length 21.8 in (55.4 cm)

79 *above*, Detail of bronze facing plate of a scabbard found at Bugthorpe. Humberside. The plate is decorated with an incised 'mat'-filled tendril motif.

81 *right*. The Witham Shield. Found in the River Witham, near Lincoln about 1826. Length 44.5 in (113 cm)

Barrow' at Arras. The horses were controlled by means of reins passing through terrets attached to a wooden yoke, though the yoke itself does not survive. Horse-bits are of iron and bronze, sometimes combining the two metals, with two or three links set between the rein rings. Many of these were finely decorated as were other bronzes designed to ornament the harness.

The picture which these Yorkshire graves present of peasant, warrior and nobility seems evident enough but elsewhere such divisions were perhaps less stark. A pit in the farm at Gussage-all-Saints, Dorset yielding débris from a bronzesmith's workshop shows that here the smith was making a range of decorated horse-bits, terrets and linch pins presumably to order. The farm at Gussage was prosperous but little else recovered from the site suggests a higher status. It is therefore difficult to gauge how far down the social scale fine metal work would have passed.

82 The Waterloo horned helmet was dredged from the River Thames near Waterloo Bridge before 1866. Height 9.6 in (24.2 cm)

83 A cemetery of square-ditched barrows during excavation at Burton Fleming, Humberside in 1975.

84 Cart-burial under excavation in 1984 at Wetwang, Humberside. The body had been interred on a dismantled cart. The iron tyres and bronze nave bands of the two wheels which had been placed flat on the ground, are clearly visible and traces of the pole can be seen running from the head to the top of the picture. Behind the body are the remains of the harness including two horsebits, an iron mirror, a bronze box decorated with Celtic Art and two linch pins. On the skeleton lay the skull and bones of a pig.

First contacts with the world of Rome

By the first century BC prehistory begins to merge, at times a little awkwardly, with historical events. Long before the Claudian invasion, Britain had resumed active trading with the Continent and had begun providing mercenaries to fight in the Gallic wars against the Roman army. Soon too refugees from these conflicts were to arrive in southern Britain. Julius Caesar was not slow to present his assaults on Britain in 55 and 54 BC as punitive expeditions against those who had helped his adversaries in Gaul, though a more compelling motivation seems to have been simply a desire for personal glory. At peace and at war then Britain had begun to meet something of the world of Rome.

By the beginning of the century trading links had been re-established between southern Britain and north-west France and a major trading post established on Hengistbury Head. Through this and other ports of entry

87 A set of bronze harness-fittings with enamel inlays from the Polden Hill hoard, Somerset. The set consists of two horsebits, four small terrets (rein rings) which would have been attached to the yoke and a larger terret probably placed on the pole. Largest terret 3.75 in (9.5 cm)

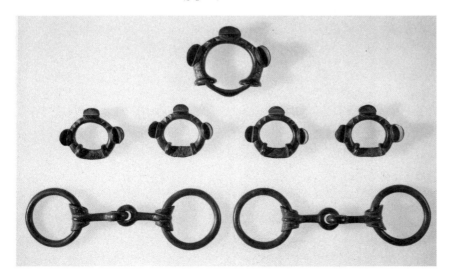

now flowed imports of a novel kind – Italian wine and the first pottery to be seen in Britain made upon the potter's wheel. In return no doubt went the corn, cattle, gold, silver, iron, hides, slaves and hunting dogs mentioned by Strabo and to these on the evidence of archaeology we should probably add salt. Along this route too were to pass refugees amongst whom Commius, Chief of the Atrebates, is known to have fled with many of his followers after his defeat in France in 52 BC to set up his capital at Silchester. With the conquest of northern France, trade also began to flow directly (during the second half of the century) into south-eastern Britain.

In the wake of these events major social changes were again in train. Many of the remaining hillforts of Wessex were in turn abandoned while in eastern England and more sporadically elsewhere a new type of settlement was being founded – the *oppida*. Though archaeologists seem more than a little unclear as to how to use this term, Caesar had no doubts for he had defeated Cassivellaunus, King of the Catuvellauni at his oppidum which may have been at Wheathampstead. Others had been created at Colchester, St Albans, Braughing, Canterbury, Silchester and Chichester. These acted as tribal centres capable of accommodating large numbers of men and livestock sometimes within imposing defensive earthworks and within them were pursued most of the activities associated with the needs of the time. Some began to mint their own coins, for coinage had been introduced to Britain in exchange for mercenaries in service across the channel, and the idea that wealth could be expressed in this form as well as helping trade began slowly to take root. It would be wrong however to see the oppida as akin to emerging towns, for though many of the features of urban life were aggregated within their boundaries, a basic lack of internal order and arrangement sets them apart.

Nor was this a time of much stability, for between Caesar's expeditions and the Claudian invasions many of the smaller tribes were either to disappear or to lose their identity within larger confederations. Stability and cohesion seem never to have been a feature of early Celtic society.

Not all the 'privileged' class, as Caesar termed it, lived within the oppida, for the custom of burying the dead had re-emerged during the first century BC and we can glimpse, through a series of rich burials scattered across south-eastern England, the range of high-class merchandise now circulating. According to Classical writers the Continental Celts enjoyed wine but had little time for Roman taste, preferring to take their liquor neat rather than diluted as was the Roman way. Nonetheless some of the apparatus associated with Roman drinking was imported. This included both bronze jugs and some of the long-handled pans used by the Romans to warm the wine before it was drunk. By the end of the century, fine Roman silver drinking cups were also reaching Britain heralding a major change in taste, for hitherto objects of silver are notably absent from prehistoric Britain. Many of these objects are clearly imported from the Roman world; other items reflect the response of the native metalsmiths to new demand. From graves at Aylesford, Kent, Baldock, Hert- 85 fordshire and Marlborough, Wiltshire come remains of wooden buckets whose metal bind-

ing strips and handle mounts are richly decorated. These too must have played an active part in drinking but whether for mixing wine or simply to hold beer is less certain, for beer as well as wine was drunk, and this from tankards made similarly of wood with metal fittings. From the blacksmith came iron firedogs used probably in pairs to help contain the fire and to support the spits upon which the joints of meat were hung, an idea taken a stage further in the frame recovered from a grave at 86 Welwyn, Hertfordshire. The iron tripod too was now in use to support a cauldron above the flames. The art of the bronzesmith was at its height. By the turn of the century sets of decorated harness trappings were being pro- 87 duced which in their inventiveness and orna-

85 This bucket was found in 1886 in a grave at Aylesford, Kent, together with a bronze jug and warming pan, three bronze brooches and pottery vessels, and had contained the cremated bones. Originally of wood, the bucket had a swing handle made of iron wrapped in bronze and was bound round with three bronze bands. Each of the three feet was decorated with a bronze plaque. The uppermost band is decorated in repoussé with patterns including pairs of stylised horses. The handle mounts are in the form of human heads. Height as reconstructed (excluding handle mounts) 11.8 in (30 cm)

ment, often incorporating enamelled inlay, now reach a new peak of attainment. But most spectacular of all are a series of bronze mirrors for these became the vehicle for the finest of all expressions of early Celtic art. In all some fourteen mirrors survive. The face was left 88 plain and polished but the back offered an unbroken surface seized upon by the artist as a field for elaborate traced and in-filled patterns often set out with great vigour by means of compasses. The handle too was cast in decorative form and in such a way as to show that when not in use the mirror would have hung upside down. Yet this was not a restful art. The eye too often is drawn to half-seen faces and disturbed by a search for symmetry which so often proves illusory. How much of the repertoire of Celtic art one wonders has been lost on human skin, for many of the patterns which bedeck these mirror backs could so easily have formed tattoos.

To this period too belongs the finest work of the goldsmiths. Amongst the more spectacular objects to survive are a series of massive gold torcs. Made to be worn around the neck, these range from sheer ostentation to works of consummate artistry like the hollow tubular torc from Broighter, Co. Derry or, finest of all, the great multi-strand torc from Snettisham, 89 Norfolk. The hoop of this torc is made of eight ropes of wire twisted together, each rope made up of eight wires similarly twisted. The massive hollow terminal rings carry lobes modelled in relief and these are coupled with complex tendrils filled with cross-hatched hurdle pattern. Such torcs represented wealth – the hoard of five torcs found at Ipswich, 90 Suffolk, weighed together no less than four and a half kilos – and presumably status, but as to who had the right to wear them we are less certain for here the evidence from the ground marries uneasily with what little written evidence has come down to us. More than one classical writer mentions torcs in connec-

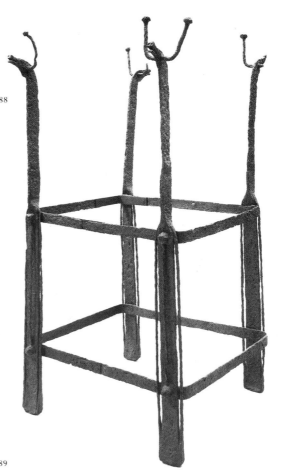

86 A wrought iron frame, the uprights of which are decorated with ox-head terminals similar to those found on contemporary fire-dogs. The frame was accompanied by other objects including five pottery amphorae, a warming pan, the handle of a bronze jug, a wooden tankard, a pair of Roman silver drinking cups and two pottery vessels. Height 56.3 in (143 cm)

88 One of the finest of the decorated bronze mirrors was found by chance at Desborough in Northamptonshire in 1908. The mirror is 13.8 in (35 cm) long.

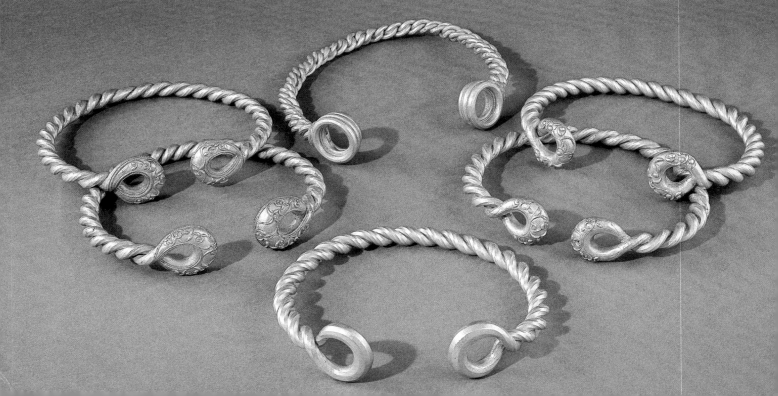

89 The great gold torc from Snettisham, Norfolk. Strictly speaking the torc is not of pure gold but an alloy of gold and silver. It was ploughed up in 1950 together with a hollow decorated gold bracelet and a small gold coin of the Atrebates. Diam. 7.8 in (19.9 cm)

90 The Ipswich Torcs. Five of the torcs were found together in 1968 on the crest of a hill at Belstead on the outskirts of Ipswich, Suffolk. The sixth, which had been disturbed by building work, was found two years later. Width of largest torc 7.75 in (19.7 cm)

91 The body of a man found during peat extraction in Lindow Moss near Wilmslow, Cheshire, dated to a late phase in the Roman period.

tion with the Celts. Polybius states that at the Battle of Telamon all the warriors in the van of the battle wore gold neckrings. But throughout the Celtic world torcs are found most often in the graves of women not warriors and these are mostly of bronze and iron not gold. Clearly torcs of gold were intended for the living not the dead and if an object of rank then the status that the torc implied was to be taken up by the next in line not consigned to the oblivion of the grave. Nor were all fearsome warriors necessarily male, for if Dio Cassius is to be believed Boudica, Queen of the Iceni, also wore a golden necklace around her regal neck.

What little can be garnered from rare stylised representations and surviving comments in early writers, such as Diodorous Siculus, Herodian and Julius Caesar, suggests that the Britons of this period wore their hair long, the males sporting a moustache. In battle, we are told they were apt to wear little besides woad, but judging by what we know of their contemporaries in Gaul, when not in

combat, coloured tunics, cloaks and trousers would have been their normal dress. It is disappointing that the only actual body to **91** have come down to us, preserved by peat was naked and dates to the first century AD. But whether a native Briton or not, here was no ordinary peasant for his nails were well manicured and he had met a violent death, first being clubbed then garrotted and his throat cut before being thrown into a shallow pool at the marsh edge, perhaps a sacrifice to some water deity. Not that all rites and rituals of the period were so orientated. From Tacitus we gather that certain groves were held sacred. For the archaeologist such statements pose problems, for if the groves were natural stands of trees and unaccompanied by man-made objects they will not be capable of detection. Fortunately more formal shrines, constructed of wood, were already being built within hillforts like Danebury and South Cadbury, and others are known from Heathrow, Hayling Island and elsewhere. Little survives from these, however, to help us piece together the rites involved or objects so connected. Shallow pointed spoons with short decorated handles, sometimes found in pairs, may be ritual objects since they serve no obvious function and one of the pair is usually pierced with a hole. So too may be a group of decorated discs from Ireland, but how or when such objects might have been employed it is impossible to say, and some may belong to the centuries following the Roman Conquest.

By the time the Roman invasion force reached Britain in AD 43, the oppidum of Colchester had become the pre-eminent port of southern Britain, controlling a major part of the trade with the Roman world. Through it came exotic imports such as Gallo-Belgic pottery from North-east Gaul; samian ware, wine **92** and olive oil from southern France and Italy and fish paste from Spain. Until recently it had been the tribal capital of the Trinovantes but

92 A group of good quality table wares which were being made in north-eastern Gaul after 15 BC, and imported in bulk into Southern England before the Roman invasion of AD 43. Found at St Albans, Hertfordshire and Colchester, Essex. Height of tallest vessel – 7.5 in (19 cm)

had now passed into the hands of the Catuvellauni, who under Cunobelinus had pursued a vigorous expansionist policy. Cunobelinus himself probably maintained friendly links with Rome but his sons Caractacus and Togodumnus were of a different stamp, anti-Roman in outlook but with the aggression of their father. With the death of Cunobelinus in AD 41 or 42 the situation must have looked to Roman eyes increasingly unstable. There could be little to lose and much to gain from well-timed intervention. Information brought back through the trading network would have confirmed that the Catuvellaunian policy had left bitter enemies amongst the neighbouring tribes, some of whom were nominally, at least, under treaty to Rome. To Claudius, who had only recently and rather surprisingly been made Emperor, an opportunity to win quick glory must have been near irresistible.

It was to a Britain divided into tribal regions, often in conflict with each other, that Aulus Plautius brought the Roman army, confident that such divisions and old enmities would work for the Roman cause. Southern Britain

was to some extent a known quantity but beyond lay regions to which Roman influence had yet to penetrate. Before long, Claudius had joined the army and ridden in triumph into Colchester to the glory which he coveted. Four years later despite stout resistance in the heavily fortified hillforts of the Durotriges a line had been established along the Fosse Way from Exeter to Lincoln. A generation later saw Wales and the North conquered, and the line taken to the Forth-Clyde. By AD 84 a final decisive victory somewhere in north-east Scotland at 'Mons Graupius' left only the Highlands unsubdued. But though the Romans had once again demonstrated the superiority of a well-marshalled fighting force over ill-organised piecemeal resistance, for many 'romanisation' was neither swift nor total. The bulk of the population living in upland Britain probably never spoke Latin nor had access to much that was not 'native'. Here, for most, life was to change little, anchored firmly upon the rock of oral tradition, responding to local needs, oblivious of imperial design. For lowland Britain life would never be the same.

Glossary

Ard A light plough which breaks the soil, but lacking a mould board does not turn a furrow.

Broch A defensive structure in the form of a circular dry stone tower tapering inwards in its upper courses.

Corbelling A technique for creating a roof in a stone-built chamber in which each of the upper courses of the wall oversails the one below so gradually reducing the span.

Dun Stone-built fort.

Hallstatt A group of iron-using communities centred on Western Czechoslovakia, Austria and Southern Germany whose influence spread rapidly to cover much of Europe by the fifth century BC.

OD Ordnance Survey Datum against which height and depths are measured.

Urnfield A widespread group of related communities practising burial by cremation in pottery urns, at first in Central and Eastern Europe later spreading to Northern and Western Europe.

Wheelhouse A stone-built circular house whose internal partition walls project inwards like the spokes of a wheel.

Further Reading

A survey of this kind must draw heavily on the work of others. I would therefore like to take this opportunity to record my thanks to all those of my colleagues whose work has contributed to the writing of this book but which cannot be acknowledged in detail. The bulk of this has been published in the national and local archaeological journals and many of the more recent discoveries have been published only in preliminary form.

Readers will find many sites described in the *Proceedings of the Prehistoric Society*, *Proceedings of the Society of Antiquaries of Scotland*, *Archaeologia Cambrensis*, in *Antiquity* and in *Current Archaeology* and in four series of monographs: *The Research Reports of the Society of Antiquaries of London* and *of the Council for British Archaeology*, *British Archaeological Reports* and the *Occasional Papers of the British Museum*.

Recent general surveys have been published by C. Renfrew (ed.) *British Prehistory – A New Outline*, Duckworth, London, 1974; J.V.S. Megaw & D.D.A. Simpson *Introduction to British Prehistory*, Leicester University Press, 1979; for agrarian developments: P.J. Fowler *The Farming of Prehistoric Britain*, CUP, 1983 and for selected social problems: R. Bradley *The Social Foundations of Prehistoric Britain*, Longman, London, 1984. Recent surveys dealing with specific phases of British Prehistory include: J.J. Wymer *The Palaeolithic Age*, Croom Helm, London, 1982; C.B. Burgess *The Age of Stonehenge*, Dent, London, 1980; B.W. Cunliffe *Iron Age Communities in Britain*, Routledge & Kegan Paul, London; 1978 (2nd ed); and I.M. Stead *Celtic Art* British Museum Publications, London 1985.

Acknowledgements

My warmest thanks must go to my colleagues Ian Stead, Ian Kinnes and Emma Myers, and to my wife Clare Longworth, for reading through the text in draft and for their many helpful suggestions; to Gillian Varndell for the immense amount of care she has taken over the selection and presentation of objects to be illustrated; to Victor Bowley for the bulk of the photographs herein reproduced; to Meredydd Moores for the time chart and map and to Valerie Ives for typing the text.

I am also grateful to the following institutions and individuals who have kindly provided photographic illustrations for the book: The Somerset Levels Project, **13**; Salisbury and South Wiltshire Museum, **18**; Irish Tourist Board, **20**; I. H. Longworth, **22**; National Museum of Ireland, **25**; G. & A. Ritchie, **26**; English Heritage 37, 74; National Monuments Record Air photograph (Crown Copyright Reserved), **38**; Wiltshire Archaeological and Natural History Society for use of **39**; A. Ritchie, **75**; and A. L. Pacitto, **83** and **84**.

Index

Illustration numbers appear in bold type